BREATHE

BREATHE

Sissel Tvedte
English Translation by Nan Lemarechal

ATHENA PRESS
LONDON

BREATHE
Copyright © Sissel Tvedte 2007
English Translation by Nan Lemarechal

ISBN 10-digit: 1 84401 912 8
ISBN 13-digit: 978 1 84401 912 0

First Published 2007 by
ATHENA PRESS
Queen's House, 2 Holly Road
Twickenham TW1 4EG
United Kingdom

Printed for Athena Press

Dedicated to my son, Tarjei, and my three grandchildren,
Signe, Vilde and Brage

Acknowledgements

Thanks to:

You, my wonderful son, Tarjei, who lifted me back into life – whose love brought me back. Who crossed almost insurmountable obstacles and who fought the battle, so to speak, alone in that little Indian hospital.

My sister, Nan, who came every day and was close to me.

Paul, who healed me.

Botolv, who read to me for hours on end, and Lis, who nursed me night and day after I came home from hospital; who washed me, dressed my wounds, bathed my feet, cooked small, tasty portions of food and tempted me to start eating again.

A warm thank you also to all of you who prayed for me and who sent love and healing.

You all helped me to come back.

'We show beauty in what we do – there are a hundred ways to kneel and kiss the ground.'

Sufi Profet

Foreword

'Write a book,' the astrologer said.

'Write? Why should I write?'

'You should write about the things you teach and how you live.'

'But so many books have been written. The world is drowning in books, everything has been written about.'

He laughed, made a gesture with his hands and said, 'Yes, but you should write simply, not filling page after page with words. It should not be an intellectual book. It must be simple. Thoughts – a flow of thoughts. Make it a book for young people, pushing them to self-evolvement. Let the book be what it is meant to be: an inspiration for some, or an alarm call; a matter of indifference to others.

'Should you irritate or provoke, it will still stir something in that person. We all walk our own paths, some unconsciously, some hesitantly. Others walk with open eyes and long strides. Bring something from your own childhood into the book. That will help others to see that we all have memories that have left scars. They will identify with the loneliness, the aloneness.'

I shook my head and said, 'I can't promise you anything. I feel no need to write. I have no time.'

He nodded again, but did not give up that easily. 'Yes. When you have written this book, you will be free. Then you can use your time to travel as much as you want.'

Not long after our talk I began to sense that the unwritten chapters of my life were becoming a burden upon my shoulders. I knew well that there was so much within me that I could share. But why? My thoughts were my own – or were they?

We exist for each other. We are all one. Each human being is a cell in the body of the earth.

Thoughts are a force, an energy that we send out. We are our thoughts. We create our lives in every second that we live; we make every second good, bad, or indifferent.

So, what about all those who do not accept this, who do not wish to receive our thoughts? Those who do not receive telepathically? Those who, for one reason or another, have closed off from that choice we all have to experience the diversity of possibilities in this life. Are they the ones I need to reach out to? Is there really a need for me to share my thoughts? Do I actually have something to share? And what about all those who come to seek me out, those who call to seek my help?

I have never encouraged anyone to do that. They come to me, and it has happened without my encouragement, as though it were my role.

So after some time had passed, I began to understand that the astrologer was correct – I would need to write this book for all of you who now read these words. Then for the second time I received a phone call from a wise being, who asked me to send light and love to you all, to give each of you the courage to live on, to help you to believe that there is a reason to go on to the destiny we all share.

And for Paul, who was here today, and was afraid of going to pieces, afraid of not being able to manage any longer – I will write with you in my heart. I will give you an insight into what is lying ahead waiting for each of us, when we become mindful of what is happening within us; when we listen, possibly for the first time, to the child within that seeks to be acknowledged.

Contents

India

'Oh, no, miss, you must not do that.'

My new Indian friend, an elderly man, looked at me with consternation. We sat on a beach in Mahalabapuram in the south of India. A palm awning, resting on three sticks, shielding us against the burning sun. It was in the middle of the day, and everything was just as it was in the beginning, before man submerged the earth. Beach and ocean stretched as far as the eye could see. There was just a cliff with a temple by the water's edge. Behind us were stretches of grass and windswept palm trees, hiding some huts further up.

The waves coming in from the Indian Ocean battered the shore and created vibrations in the air.

'A woman must never do that!' he continued patiently. 'A woman must never touch a man's leg here in India.' He had brought a collection of Indian gods, beautifully carved in stone, to the beach. He opened the parcels carefully and lovingly, one after another. With great care he put the worn newspaper aside in a box, and told me about the many goddesses of India.

We had been sitting there for a time in silence looking at the ocean, and I had another question for him, pointing to one of the figures. 'And this one, what was her name? I have forgotten it.' I had pushed his leg with my foot in order to catch his attention again.

Now I felt ashamed because I had not been aware enough of this country's customs. A horde of us coming here from the West was invading an ancient culture with our ways. We were bathing in our small bathing suits and had spread ourselves out on the beach in order to obtain some of the venerated golden colour. The women in India bathe, when possible, away from where they can be watched by the men. They take off their saris, rinse them in the water, and spread them over the bushes to dry in a couple of minutes. Then they bathe in long underskirts and blouses. They bathe to cleanse themselves.

'I am sorry. I didn't know that. Thank you for telling me.' I smiled at him apologetically, and he nodded back, seriously.

'Please, tell me more,' I asked him.

He told me about Ganesha the elephant god, who represents the ultimate wisdom; about Shiva with the three faces, and Parvati, his wife; about Brahma and Vishnu.

As he spoke I listened to his voice, to the sounds in the air, to the gods.

My eyes were caught by a crab rushing over the beach, and I watched it disappear into a hole in the sand. Sun, beach, ocean... I felt one with everything.

I *am*, we *are* – time had abruptly stopped.

Why did I go to India?

As time passed it became a certainty. I had to go. India was pulling me to her.

When I was sixteen, I met a middle-aged man from India at a party. He showed a special interest in me, and watched me for quite a while before asking to see my hand. I shivered a little, as it seemed a bit scary, but I showed it to him anyway.

'You have much from our culture in you,' he said. He was wise enough not to say more, but he invited me to India and gave me his address. He asked me to write to his wife. He had no time to write himself, but knew that she would appreciate it. 'That way you will learn to know our country's culture,' he explained, 'and will have greater pleasure when you come to visit.'

I did not follow it up. I wrote one letter and got a long, nice letter back, and it filled me with joy and gratitude that she, a busy, grown-up, woman, showed me so much attention and kindness.

Anyway, it rested there. Other considerations filled my sixteen-year-old head. The letter lay there, the answer postponed again and again. So much time passed by that it became embarrassing. I put it out of my thoughts and the address got lost.

Many years later, when I was in Sweden, India emerged again.

I was in a commune there, following a course in rebirthing, and met a bunch of enthusiastic people who had just come back from a trip to an ashram in India. That evening for the first time I heard about the mahavatar Babaji, Shri Herakhan Baba, who lived in the Kumaon Mountains in Uttar Pradesh in the foothills of the Himalayas.

They talked about him with enthusiasm, about his love and wisdom and his teaching, which was love, peace and simplicity, but I was not interested. 'What do I need him for?' I asked. 'I have Jesus Christ.'

'Yes, but there is no contradiction. In the temples of Herakhan there are also pictures of Jesus. Babaji does not belong to any definite religion, but respects them all. Go there yourself and meet him. Then you will understand. He teaches that which the church has forgotten.'

I didn't want to talk about him any more, and asked why we sang '*Om Namaha Shivaya*' for hours. The night before, we had sat and sung it over and over for two hours.

'This mantra is the strongest,' I was told. 'It means the highest intelligence, the greatest love; God. Christ, the Holy Spirit, Shiva. Yes, it is a greeting in the honour of the gods, of the highest masters. It hails the divine in man.'

I had been singing with them for an hour and my throat was dry. I can't stand this anymore, I thought. I don't want to sing any longer. I can decide for myself. But I was told that I pulled energy out of the group by being passive. What we did by singing this mantra was to build up energy.

It took some time for me to understand that there was a resistance in me, filling me with restlessness, and that there was a blockage in my throat that made it so dry. During the following days I had several instruction sessions when I learned how to breathe deeply and correctly, and after a week I was able to sing freely and strongly from an open-throat chakra.

Babaji was working with me before I even met him, and without my wishing it. At least I had no conscious wish for his intervention and knew little of what lay ahead for me, and the sort of relationship I would have with Babaji; but after a couple of weeks back in Norway he appeared clearly in a dream and asked me to come to his temple.

Coincidences – do they exist? I don't think so. But it is up to us to be conscious, to work with ourselves, teaming with ourselves to allow new opportunities to be born.

At this time, I was working as a silversmith and enamel painter and had been invited to the world fair in Basle in Switzerland to demonstrate the secrets of enamel art. I knew that one of Babaji's temples was situated in the Alps, not far from Basle. This was my opportunity to go to the temple and find out more. I felt compelled to discover what was there for me.

It was a warm autumn day, so I had dressed lightly. I took the train from Basle as far as possible and then a taxi as far as the road went. Then the mountain stood before me – I would have to travel the rest of the way on foot. I carried a written description of the road I was to follow and an indication of how long the journey might take. I had begun early and should have had ample time to reach my destination before dark.

A couple of hours later, the sky became suddenly darker and a cold draught fell from the mountains as the year's first snow began to swirl around me. It fell quietly, as quietly as snow does, but this snow was dense. My steps became heavier and it became increasingly difficult to see the track as it disappeared under a thick blanket of white fluff. I advanced more and more slowly, the snow got deeper and it started to get dark. A part of me wanted to turn back to safety, but it was too late to turn around.

'Dear God, help me to find the way,' I prayed. 'Help me to get there before it gets totally dark. Thank you for hearing me and for being with me.'

Then suddenly I had to stop. The track went in two directions. Right? Left? Which one should I follow? My directions did not mention crossroads, and the wrong path could possibly be fatal. I stretched out my arms, one towards the right and one towards the left, and closed my eyes.

I asked my guardian angel, whom I always feel close to, to take one of my hands and guide me to the correct track. Soon I felt my right arm pointing me in the desired direction. Gratefully I sent my thanks, and continued my trek up the mountain, muttering '*Om Namaha Shivaya*' with each new breath.

Just before it was totally dark I begun to see faint outlines ahead: the temple, the ashram and several small huts. This day had been a powerful reminder that I did not walk the road alone.

Later, during a deep meditation in the safety of the ashram, Babaji appeared to me once more, this time indicating that he was together in spirit with Jesus. They were both surrounded by a golden aura, and I understood for the first time that Babaji, like Jesus before him, was now showing me the way just as Jesus had done during his time on earth.

I understood then that I was one of his disciples, that I had known him before, and that there was no contradiction between Jesus and Babaji. They both stand for God, love and the way. I decided that day that I would go to Herakhan, in India, to meet this teacher who lived in the foothills of the Himalayas. I wanted to go to the master who lived in peace, love and simplicity.

After I returned home, my husband and I went to see an Indian film, where I totally connected with what I saw on the screen. I knew this place, and those were my mountains. Tears ran down my face and I felt uplifted and happy. I was there, feeling and smelling the scents of nature. When the film ended I just sat, unable to move or to say a word. My husband softly shook my shoulder.

'Sissel, we have to leave, the film has ended.'

It took some time, but at last I managed to pull myself together and follow him out.

'I have to go there,' I said. 'I have to go to India. I have been there before.'

Not long afterwards I began my journey.

The Journey

I went to India alone.

This was my pilgrimage. I had to go back, because a part of me belonged to this part of the world. I wanted to go back to find more of myself, to see more clearly all these pictures which kept emerging in my consciousness. It was time to put them together.

I had developed a spiritual contact with Babaji. He helped me when I called on him, in the same way as I was helped when I prayed to God, to Jesus and to my angel.

My eyes were filled with tears when my plane landed in New Delhi. I had come home. Deep warmth filled my stomach. I could have kissed the dusty, dirty ground, but I just knelt and put my hands flat on the ground, hailing Mother India.

I talked with the porters, the drivers, with the people around me, filled with a feeling of happiness I could not explain. I knew everything, even the poverty did not affect me. It did not make me sad because I knew it. I remembered all the good things, the simple life, the solidarity between those of us who were living together then, in the life I was so brutally torn away from. India, my country – my people. I understood why I had felt so insecure and homeless as a little girl. I remember asking my father, 'Are you sure that I am your child?'

I took a taxi to an address I had been given by friends in Norway, dined on rice and beans with the Indian family who lived there, crawled under the mosquito net and slept. I slept for fourteen hours, until a voice singing outside my door woke me up.

'Mangoes, bananas, apples, oranges!'

He would not stop. Again and again he sang his litany outside my hut, and I had to give up, open my eyes to the sunlight and greet the day. I bought fruit and had my first breakfast in India, on sandy ground surrounded by palms, flowering bushes and inquisitive little monkeys.

I stayed there for two days, breathing India in through all my pores, and made new friends. I met an American woman who had come down from Daramsala. She was working for the Dalai Lama and was teaching Tibetan children at the school there. Now she was in New Delhi with a patient, a nun who had been bitten by a poisonous snake and was lying semi-conscious in a very small hospital close by. The nun had gangrene in her right arm and was not certain to survive.

Then I made the fatal mistake I so intently tell others not to make: I offered to give her healing without her having asked me to. I was so full of energy and so eager to serve, I forgot Rule Number One in healing – *the patient must ask for it*. When we practise healing, we pull in the life energy from the universe, from God, and we work with that energy to pull the sickness out of the other person's body. Often the patient has no contact with his or her higher will, and does not know clearly if they want to be healed or not.

I was sure that the nun wanted to get well, and so I took over. I worked with her for a long time, and pulled the illness out of her body by stroking the aura. I felt a coldness coming over me as the warmth returned to her face, so I knew I had pulled it out of her. Then I put my hands upon her and prayed that she be filled with energy and light from the universe of love, from God.

When I had finished I had goose pimples all over my body and I felt rather sick. There was no water to cleanse myself with, and I had forgotten to throw away the negative things I had pulled from my patient. I felt icy cold in the blinding heat, went back to my night quarters and slept for another twelve hours.

The next day I travelled by bus towards the Himalayas and Herakhan. For me this journey seemed like a voyage through several lives, I was in a meditative state, but at the same time I registered everything as sharply as if the day's events had been recorded on film.

It was sunny. It was hot. The bus was overloaded with people and packages, bags and boxes of all sorts. There was even room in the middle of everything for an intricately wrought hen coop made of cane. Fortunately the bus had only a couple of remaining glass panels, so it did not get unbearably hot, but soon a thin layer of dust covered everything. I had brought my usual snack with me from home, a mixture of raisins, almonds and rolled oats. Now and then I took a mouthful and chewed it for a long time, not only thirty-six times, maybe a hundred. That took the hunger away and helped me resist the temptations which were offered at each stop. Norwegian stomachs need a long time to adapt to Indian food.

I wanted to share my impressions of the journey, and I tried to talk to one after another of my fellow passengers in English, but I found nobody who could communicate in this language. I had to talk with gestures and eyes. By the time I reached New Delhi I discovered that the belief that all Indians speak English was a fallacy. Outside the main towns, it was even worse, so I concentrated totally on all there was to see.

People were walking in both directions along the road and almost everyone was carrying something. They carried their loads on their heads: big, long bundles of wood, bags filled with rice, brass or clay jars filled with water, enormous, wide baskets of fruit and vegetables. Everything was beautifully arranged ready for sale.

They impressed me, all these beautiful, graceful people with their proud bearing. They looked as if they could carry anything anywhere. Often a woman carried a small child on her hip as well, and led another by the hand. They were dressed in colourful saris and they lit up the landscape and made me think of butterflies. It was pure joy to rest my eyes on them.

The bus thundered on. Traffic was dense in both directions.

Horns were used frequently by most of the drivers as they turned away from oncoming cars with unbelievable precision, often just some inches before the big blast.

'Horn please' was written across the back of the enormous trucks, a request which seemed entirely superfluous as everybody honked their horns to their hearts' contents, whether it was to overtake or for whatever reason.

Carts pulled by oxen moved resolutely on at their own pace. In between all these people and vehicles, heavily-loaded donkeys tripped on their way to and from New Delhi.

Hens, pigs and goats jumped away from the car tyres, but the people living by the roadside did not seem to notice the traffic. They sat outside their tiny sheds repairing machines, cars and bicycles, cooking their food, or drinking milk and tea by the roadside. Some slept on beds, others directly on the ground. Some sat by their sewing machines making clothes, others played cards, and the children worked or played. Everything happened right beside the long, straight road, sheltered at intervals by majestic trees and running north-east towards the Himalayas. Sheds were also built along the roadside and the fields behind them lay deserted, scorched by the sun. I wondered why people didn't prefer to pull back from the road, the noise and the exhaust fumes, but an Indian told me later that because of the wild animals the safest place was by the road.

Here, as everywhere else in India, the cows have right of way. If a cow crosses the road or decides to lie down for a rest in the middle of it, all the vehicles either stop or make a careful detour round it.

In the middle of all these teeming multitudes there was still a peace and a harmony. Although the cars hurried along, it seemed that everybody had the time they needed. People appeared untouched by all that happened around them. They had ready smiles and laughter, and they crowded around me when we got out of the bus. People touched my arm carefully to get my attention. They talked, laughed and gesticulated. I was met with friendliness and openness everywhere.

In India I saw trucks and buses decorated with wreaths on their bonnets, showing they had been blessed by the morning's *arathi*, and almost every vehicle had its little god figure over the dashboard, decorated with flowers and incense sticks. Maybe this is why there are comparatively few accidents in this multitude of traffic.

We never stopped for long, ten minutes at most, then into the bus again. The journey lasted a long time; the trip went on from early morning until darkness fell. At last there was nothing to see except the lights from oncoming vehicles and small fires outside sheds here and there along the road. The people around me were asleep, and after a while I leaned over my bag and let myself be rocked to sleep too.

I was alone, all by myself, just my big backpack and me. I was surrounded by night, dense black Indian night, the darkness broken only by a single light bulb hanging from the roof. The bus had stopped, the engine was turned off and all the passengers had left. Now the driver was also leaving. I tried to speak to him in English, to no avail. He just made a gesture of despair, shook his head from side to side, and he too disappeared into the darkness. It was evident that the bus had reached its destination – and it was without doubt night. I was filled with unease. What now, Sissel? What do we do now?

'It is completely safe for a grown woman to travel alone in India if you only dress like they do. Cover yourself with a shirt long enough to cover your behind, wear a long skirt or trousers and a shawl. But you must never be outside alone when it is dark. Women are supposed to be inside then.' These words from an old India traveller some months earlier suddenly rang in my ears. But what could I do about it?

In front of me was a shed filled with crates, where some men were sitting drinking tea. A long plank served as a counter and a man boiled water and milk on a stove made out of an old oil drum. Some half-grown boys ran around barefoot, playing and laughing among the crates, and occasionally helping to bring twigs for the fire and serve tea.

Resolutely I took my backpack and left the bus. I installed myself on one of the crates, pushed it towards a pole, put the backpack behind my back as support and made myself as comfortable as possible. This could be a long wait. I took some raisins and almonds from my pocket and chewed them for a long, long time.

All my movements were watched intently, and I knew they were being commented on. The men watched me with big eyes, just as small children would do at home. Was it confidence, or a sense of security? They did not try to hide their curiosity or camouflage their thoughts as we usually do in our part of the world, and when I registered that it made me feel touched and safe. No, I was not afraid, but in a way I felt trapped.

There was no traffic; the road did not continue any further. I had seen no cars or vehicles of any sort for the last hour. Where on earth was I? According to my calculations. I should have arrived long ago. My map was no use to me. It had been pitch dark on the bus for the last few hours and I had not been able to read it, and the signpost beside the shed was written in Indian letters which I could not decipher.

I looked up towards the sky, towards the vault of heaven with its bright stars. I was looking for my own star, the one that I had connected with as a small child as if it was there to look after me; and there it was again. It was like a sign just above me, like a promise, as if it said, 'I am with you.'

Consciously I started my karma yoga breathing, deep, full inhaling. Each time I breathed in I repeated God's name, and sometimes the old mantra, *Om Namaha Shivaya*. Each time I breathed out I let go of all thought. Then I asked my invisible angel, who had helped me before, to send me a person who could speak English. After that I sent a thank you for the help I knew I was going to get. I felt blessed and taken care of.

An hour passed, and then a man emerged from the darkness. With determined steps he came right up to me, stopped with an open smile and said, 'Hello, miss, where are you from?'

He seemed delighted to hear that I had come all the way from Norway, even though he had no clear idea of where it really was. Up there where it is always cold, he suggested, almost at the North Pole. I drew maps on small pieces of paper that I pulled from my bag, trying to explain, and he laughed happily when he understood that I had come all this way to be in Herakhan, to worship his Baba.

'Our Baba, Herakhan Baba.' He told everyone around us about me, then he bought me a big mug of tea and we drank together, two new friends. Although who knows, maybe we were friends in earlier times? It felt like that.

The world was a good place to be. The darkness was dense around us. The air was filled with sounds of the night; insects, animal cries from the jungle and a low murmur from the men around us.

Life was here and now. There was no rush. I sent kind thoughts to my home: I am well. I send you light and love. I was on my way to my temple, my future residence for half a year. Everything was as it should be.

My friend told me that I had gone a bit astray. I had taken the wrong bus, but in an hour and a half another bus would arrive. It would take me to the little town where I was to meet Shri Muni Raji and then decide how best to go on.

'But you must not go to any hostel. That is no place for you. There are nasty animals that would bite you. You would not like that. You must stay on the bus till it gets light.'

He bought me another mug of tea, but refused to let me pay for it this time.

'No. It is an honour to buy it for you. You have come this long way to worship our Baba, we are proud of that.' He showed me so much kindness, I was profoundly touched and I was almost melancholy saying goodbye to him when the night bus arrived.

It seemed impossible to find room for both me and my backpack on this already overloaded vehicle. There were crates, sacks, bundles and people outside and in, but he pushed me inside somehow. I just managed to turn and saluted him, '*Om Namaha Shivaya.*' He put his hands together in front of his face, bowed and responded, then disappeared into the darkness. I was on my way again.

Cool night air caressed my cheeks – there were no glazed windows in this bus either. I was shaken back and forth, but we were so tightly packed together that I managed to sit quite firmly. It had been a long day and the clatter was sleep-inducing, so I soon fell asleep among the bundles, buckets and other sleeping people.

At last we were emptied out of yet another bus, but this time I knew I had come to the right place. I felt dead tired and could not resist the temptation of trying to find a bed, so I looked for someone who spoke English and found a 'hotel' for the rest of the night. It cost fifty rupees for the room and a shower. That was about twelve Norwegian crowns, not an outrageous price, but what it bought me was not luxury. A room and a bed, with a sheet that had been used many times, and a 15-watt light bulb that was meant to light up both the bedroom and the 'bathroom' behind. The bathroom had a hole in the floor, a water tap and a bucket.

I looked at the bed and cared about little else. To sleep, that would be wonderful. I threw myself on the bed, but got up again just as quickly.

'Who is there?'

A small animal was on its way toward the bed. Oh, no! I grabbed my torch from the side pocket of my backpack and directed the light beam towards it. Yes, it was a scorpion. What now? Could scorpions climb? No, I realised, they couldn't, not up iron legs anyway. I dared to go down to the floor for a moment. I pulled the bed out from the wall and hurried back onto it, taking a sweater and an anorak from the top of my pack and covering myself with them. There were no blankets here, the mattress was thin and hard, and the pillow felt like a sandbag. I pushed it down to my comrade on the floor and fell half asleep, dozing with one eye open.

It was difficult to keep my eyes off the scorpion. It wandered around the room, along the wall, again and again, in a circular movements which finally sent me to sleep in spite of my wish to stay in control. I surrendered myself to my angel once again, making the transition, meeting with another world.

I woke up. Bright rays of sunshine forced their way through the shutters, through all the chinks around the door and through the wide opening underneath it. There was no sign of my friend from the night before.

I bent over the side of the bed, picked up one of my shoes, shook it and looked carefully into it. Then went through the same procedure with the other before I put them on and went into the bathroom. I was met by ten to fifteen cockroaches, greeting me good morning. Child's play, I told myself, they won't bite. I filled a bucket with water and poured it over myself. It was good to get rid of some of the dust from the bus trip. I returned to my pack, pulled out a towel and had a good rub down to get warm and dry. Then I emptied the pack very carefully, shaking each garment and putting it on the bed. No, there was no scorpion there. Maybe it had had its fill of cockroaches and gone home to its wife and children...

I shivered a little, thinking of the nun in New Delhi who had gangrene after her encounter with the snake. I remembered that there were many sorts of scorpions, not all equally dangerous, but I felt it was not good for my health to have too close a meeting with any one of them.

The journey continued. I went to Shri Muni Raji's house to get information about how and when to find my way to Herakhan. I did not find him there, but met two Germans instead. They had been waiting two days. The road we were supposed to take had been washed away. It had rained for several days and the river had grown big and powerful. There was a flood, impossible to get through for several weeks.

We got information about the road to another of Baba's temples. Chilianola in Nainital District, and were told to go there. Reluctantly, we left; we were so near our original destination and yet unable to reach it.

Another bus, looking as if it could fall apart any minute, but defying all the odds, took us up into the mountains in a cloud of black smoke. I watched the young German girl, Susanne. I knew her from somewhere, sometime, and again I felt a closeness. She turned towards me and smiled, and I could see that she thought the same thing. We were friends who had met again.

The bus suddenly stopped on its way up the hill. There were no houses here, no people, but by the roadside there was a big stone with a small altar and a picture of Babaji. Incense was burnt and we said, '*Om Namaha Shivaya*,' and we were all given marks on our foreheads. Again I had this feeling of being home. I felt no need to talk, simply to exist.

The meeting with the ashram gave me the same feeling of belonging. Here were people from many countries, but only a few from Scandinavia – a couple of Swedes and me from Norway. I was the first to come from there, I was told. I shared a room with Susanne and two girls from Switzerland. Our room had a concrete floor, an unglazed window with iron bars, and a door with a solid iron lock. We were told to be sure to lock and bolt the door when we went to bed at night.

Only two weeks earlier they had had a visit from a tiger during the night. Someone had forgotten to lock the big wrought iron gate of the ashram, and the temptation had been too great for the uninvited guest. It had killed and half eaten one of the dogs in the ashram; but a couple of weeks earlier it had taken a small child from the village.

From that first day, the remaining dog found its way to me,

appointing itself as my lifeguard. Its care for me was very touching. It followed me wherever I went and stationed itself outside
my door at night. I was not allowed to bring it inside, nor into the
temple, contrary to the custom in Switzerland. There they had
four small Tibetan temple dogs always present during *arathi*. They
sat quietly like statues all through the service, until at the end of it
there was a distribution of sweets. Then they moved along the
rows, sat down and begged chocolate from us.

It was good to have arrived, to settle down. I felt an intense
desire to lie down on my sleeping bag, even if it was just for an
hour, but there was lots to do and the day was already well
advanced. We each received a thin mattress filled with grass, and
set them out in a row as best we could.

In New Delhi I had bought two saris with a blouse and
underskirt. It would soon be time for the evening's *arathi*, and the
journey had left visible traces, so we went to the washroom to
have a thorough wash. There was a tap on the wall and buckets,
but the water here was deliciously warmed by the sun, and even
though we had been told to use water carefully, we used several
buckets. I was filled with a sense of solemnity as I walked in my
new sari to the temple and our first *arathi*.

Outside there were long rows of sandals, and inside the
temple was already half full. It was an incredibly beautiful, simple
temple, with marble floor and walls, the women sitting on the left
side, the men on the right. On the altar stood a figure of Baba,
and along the walls were pictures and symbols from all the
world's religions. I was filled with joy and gratitude. Even if I did
not get to Herakhan, I had still come home. Again I felt part of
something familiar, something wonderfully light, strong and
meaningful.

The bells tolled. An enormous drum was beaten, and the
sound vibrations filled every cell in my body, streamed out of the
fifteen-square-metre opening of the temple and spread down the
mountainside to the valley beneath us.

Song filled the temple, clear and strong. We sat on the floor,
close together, with the tiny children crawling over us and around
us. I was overwhelmed with emotion, and warm tears filled my
eyes. I was there with every pore of my being, my body pleasantly

heavy and my breathing harmonious. The songs were familiar and dear, just as they had been in the Swiss Alps.

The days started early in the ashram. At three o'clock in the morning I was already in line at the washroom in order to throw the morning's bucket of water over myself. It was dark, and now the water was icy cold. The warmth would come back later.

After I had dressed, I pulled a blanket around my shoulders and went to the morning's darshan, which means to meet a holy person and get a blessing. We were each given four yellow stripes across the forehead and a red and yellow mark on the third eye, the point above the nose, between the eyes, as well as a couple of grains of rice in the same place. There was total silence: we did not talk much there. We lived in karma yoga, in silent worship, and gave thanks to the Lord.

It was still dark when we walked together to puja, another place in the grounds of the ashram, where a big fire was burning. We sat around it and sang, threw grains of rice into the flames and prayed for all those who needed it and for peace and love among all human beings.

The light was coming. The sun coloured the mountain tops around us first pink, then shining white. The experience of beauty was overwhelming.

After puja came the morning's *arathi*, the service of light at seven o'clock. Later still it was time for breakfast, warm, sweet tea and biscuits or a sandwich that we bought in the tiny little shop outside the ashram wall. Now it was possible to talk, for those who wished to. There were things to share, especially for those who were meeting again after months and years of separation, but mostly there was silence. Most people sought silence and came here for that reason. In the silence God talks to us, and in the silence we can listen to the voice of our own souls.

When I was quite young I had learnt this at home. 'In silence and trust your strength shall be.'

Silence is good for those who dare to be present in themselves, in their own deep centre.

Now we worked in the ashram and the garden. We were allocated chores according to our knowledge and skill: some helped to build a new library, others did the cleaning and the washing, worked in the garden, did masonry work and repaired buildings. As a silversmith and enamel painter, I was given the task of decorating the ornaments on the temple door and the statues outside. They quickly became worn and weather-beaten in this harsh climate.

It was rewarding work, and while I did it I met many Indians who came to visit the temple. After a couple of days I was asked if I would stand in for the priest during the hours he was at home having meals. Another joy had been given me. I could sit in the temple and meditate when there were no visitors, and I was there to welcome those who came, and give them blessing and marks on their forehead. This was something I was familiar with. People who saw me there barefoot and clad in my sari assumed I was someone from the north of India, and from the day I shaved my hair off, this impression became even stronger.

Some years ago everybody had to shave their heads to live in this ashram. Now it is a matter of choice, but after some weeks I felt the need to do it. It was said that by doing this we shed the old ways; it was a kind of cleansing.

It was a free, good feeling.

On the way back from the barber I had the experience of being greeted as 'the old Tibetan master'. I was greeted with a deep bow, and it made me think back to something that had happened two years earlier. I had seen myself in Tibet, once as a boy of six or seven years, another time as a yogi.

It happened during a so-called 'regression' – going back to previous lives. Back in our room at the ashram, I picked up a mirror and saw the yogi again. He had appeared in me, and my face was his face.

In Chilianola the weeks passed in work and in worshipping God in gratitude and prayer. It was good to be there and I felt free.

I was getting used to the big spiders on the ceiling. We talked about them as we lay in our sleeping bags. What if they let themselves fall down on us during the night? We were told that they were not poisonous, but they were not very tempting bedfellows. For the first few nights I turned over on my side and pulled the sleeping bag well over my head, to be on the safe side.

But you get used to most things, and I soon learned to lie safely on my back with my sleeping bag open, drifting into the world of sleep with the spiders dangling silently over me.

One day some people came over from Herakhan to help with the work in Chilianola. Soon there would be a big celebration, and Shri Muni Raji wanted everything to be ready and as nice as possible. The road had been repaired. Suzanne and I wanted to go to Herakhan, our original destination, at once, but we were asked to wait another couple of weeks. They needed us here.

Most of my time was now occupied with healing the sick. More and more people had arrived at the ashram, and there were now eight in our little room. That was just about all it would take, and we lay there like sardines, but the days were long and we slept like logs when we were in there.

I often forgot to rinse myself off after having done healing work. There were too many people there.

One morning I felt very weak and understood that I had to slow down. It was my turn to recuperate. I kept myself quiet, but could not refuse when I was asked to go to a man who was very weak. I worked with him for an hour and returned to my room, deciding to stand firm. I knew I had to rest.

This worked for a while, then I was called for again. This time it was a child, the daughter of the Italian woman who lived in a room just beside ours. The little girl had dysentery and was very ill.

A child is more important than I am. I forgot to ask the advice of my angel, and once again I thought, The others are more important than me, I can manage. I went to the girl, gave her healing, and as if this were not enough, I added a prayer:

'Lord, let me take this on myself. Let this little girl get well.'

My prayer was heard. But only minutes later, on my way back to my room, I fainted. I threw up and the diarrhoea flowed. Friends came running and washed my face with cold water. I was conscious for a while, and they wanted to get me on my feet, but it was impossible; my legs wouldn't hold me and I fell down again. They tried to carry me into my room and knelt down around me. One of the biggest and heaviest of my helpers was unfortunate enough to put the full weight of his knee on my right wrist. There was a loud crack, and my wrist was dislocated.

I had succumbed to everything I had been healing others for, my doctors later discovered. Now I was really sick, so sick that I did not know day from night and could not answer any questions. Once when I was conscious, I asked after the little girl and was told, 'She is well, she is out playing.'

I lost consciousness again. I lay there for another week, until they dared not keep me there any longer. I was sent in a taxi to New Delhi, accompanied by two women who were going back home to Germany.

Death

The journey down through the hills on the long road to Delhi was horrible.

I had to lie with my knees bent on the small back seat, too weak to even move, with the result that my knees were damaged too. Infection ravaged my body. Every joint screamed in pain. I could not drink without the liquid coming up again immediately, or being discharged the other way. I had been incapable of keeping food down since that first day when I fainted. I had an amoebic infection in my bowels.

The times when I lost consciousness were wonderfully liberating. During these episodes I saw pictures and heard the most wonderful music. I felt blessed and knew I was being taken care of. I had contact with my angels and with the universe. I understood that this was something I had to go through and work through and live through all by myself. I had to manifest my own will to stay in this world, to get on with my evolution.

I had to go into the pain and work through it.

Day followed day with unbearable pain. I had neither sleep nor rest, except when I was unconscious.

I was admitted to a small Indian hospital where they did not have the medication I needed. Nor did they have saline intravenous liquid. My lungs were straining to obtain enough oxygen but it was no longer possible to breathe. My lungs were filling with water because of blood poisoning and the high fever. I was given sweetened liquid intravenously, which did not improve my condition. Lying flat on my back without a pillow, I was about to drown in my own lung fluid – lung oedema.

At times I felt time had stopped. When I was conscious, I looked at the clock on the wall but the minute hand did not move. The same nurse came in and did the same thing over and over again. She held a syringe in her hand, held it up towards the light, put the needle into my arm and suddenly was gone. She came in again, the same thing happened. The clock still showed the same time.

I felt locked in, locked in my own prison. My physical body kept me imprisoned; I couldn't stand it any longer. I was experiencing torture without release, night and day, day and night.

Wasn't it in hell where time stood still? I felt this was where I was. How wonderful, I imagined, it would be to be able to die.

The pain almost drove me mad. There were no painkillers. My will to fight was diminishing. Maybe I was not meant to live. At home they could manage without me. We had had many good years together – I could go on in another body, after a break on the other side. I did believe in reincarnation and rebirth, after all.

My son was an adult now and had finished his education, and my husband was immersed in his work and his own life. My students and my clients would manage without me. We are all dispensable. We spend some time here on earth, live out our karma and our destiny as best we can and go on to the next task.

After I had finished thinking this through, there was nothing more to hold me back. I floated out of my body, away from the hospital and out into the universe. I saw the world beneath me and suddenly I was standing outside my own house in Norway, looking into the living room through the garden door. I said goodbye, giving thanks for everything life had given me.

What potential we have, what enormous strength we possess...

As soon as I had said my goodbyes, the nameplate fell off my mailbox and all the light bulbs at the front of the house and all the way down to the mailbox went out. A second later the light bulbs on the other side of the house and down to the road all went out simultaneously. My dog and my cat were both in the living room, and were running around desperately. Varga was barking like mad and Chat Noir was meowing and screaming wildly.

My friend, Lis, who was looking after my house while I was away, was thinking, Something terrible must be happening to Sissel.

I heard a voice asking, 'Are you willing to stay on earth?'

'I don't know,' I replied. 'I have done my work. I would so much like to come home.'

'You are still needed.'

'Yes? Well, if that is my higher will.'

'Are you willing, even if you have to lose your right arm?'

I looked down at my arm, which hung dead, swollen and bluish by my side. Then I straightened myself and answered 'Yes.'

In that same second I was back in my bed at the hospital, and the pain invaded me again.

Stay in my body? Be here, yes – but how to get well again?

I was just lying there; there was nobody who could help me. No one spoke English and they had no medication to give me.

I discovered that my senses had widened out. I could look through the walls of the hospital.

I was only partly there; it was difficult to stay in the present, it was good to get away from the pain and the hospital.

I had bedsores as well, the bed I was lying on was very hard, but it made no difference; my situation could not get any worse.

Again I floated away. I could not control it.

I was in the middle of a fire. I was being burned, together with many others. We were tied together, connected by a deep affection and a love so deep we could not hate our executioners. I knew we were dying for our faith, and my thoughts were seeking God. We had chosen to die rather than deny our faith.

The smoke burned my throat and the horrible stench of burnt hair, flesh and excrement filled my head. I had to remain clear-headed and I prayed. I had to find the pearl, the light, God.

I held the light in my hands. It was like a shining pearl. The flames were licking around us, but before I could die from the flames I was choked to death by the smoke.

Then I was in the light.

For a brief moment, everything was light.

I knew the answer to all things, the riddle of the world was solved, the universe was open. The colours were pure, clear, and transparent. I was looking inwards, ever inwards.

The deep wisdom was enchanting. The space around me was violet blue, like velvet. The light streamed toward me, sparkling, shining light. It was too strong for my eyes, but the light embraced me, blessing me and greeting me.

I knew that I belonged here, that I too was light, and I lifted my hand to the side, towards the space. Flowers sprang from all my fingers, they glowed against the dark deep violet infinity.

I created life. I moved my hand and the flowers became butterflies. They flew out into space like glowing beings with colours I no longer had any words for. At the same time I saw and experienced people on the earth.

Where my thoughts went I could see everything, their thoughts, their feelings, their destinies. Words were so insufficient; I had no language for this. Everything *is*, and I *am*. There is nothing more to wish for. I am one with all, and all is love and wisdom.

To be pulled back was exceedingly painful. I could not bear it and floated away again, this time to a choking darkness. I was sucked down with an insane, unreal speed, but somehow it seemed natural.

I was in the interior of the earth. How did I know? I knew everything. It was dark, darker than the night. Was it hell? No.

Was it emptiness? No.

Was it loneliness? Yes, above everything it was lonely. A deep loneliness surpassed everything. The deep despair that invaded me was unbearable and seemed to last for ever.

'God, where are you?' I cried. 'My spiritual beings, do you exist? My guardian angel, where have you gone?'

No answer but chilling silence. Nothing broke the darkness, the oppressive silence. It sank in towards me, capturing me.

'No, no. God! Take me back, help me! My soul, my light, hold me, lift me.'

And the light shines in the darkness.

The words came to me, and in that instant I knew I could bear everything because I believed in the light, in God. I knew that life and death had a meaning, that I was walking my way back to the light through darkness. I called on my soul and my light.

'I seek refuge in the Lord.'

And in thin, thin bands the light came… first slowly, then more rapidly. Bands of light reached my inner eye and I was lifted, filled with soft music.

Now I was rising toward the light, and it grew stronger.

Everything became golden. I moved, floating on a soft carpet of light. I had beings, people around me.

I am.

I was met with an immense light.

I bowed in yearning, joy, and humility. I saw a double column – light thrown out from light. This was where I came from. This was where I belonged, here with God, the creator of the universe.

Nothing was missing. Everything was filled with love. I had no thought, no yearning. All was in me. I was in God.

Life

'Your son is coming.'

'Your son is coming from Norway.'

'Your son is here.'

My son? But I was no longer alive. It was not possible to come back. I had said goodbye. They could manage without me. It was not necessary for me to return, I did not wish it. It was lonely on earth, and my time there was over. My work was ended.

Flashes of pain grabbed me again, chasing through my body. My body? I was back in my sick, miserable body.

A hand touched me.

'Mamma, Mamma, I am here. It is Tarjei.'

With an enormous effort I managed to open my eyes. The boy with the golden hair, was this my son?

I am sorry. I have to leave you. I love you, but I am not here any longer. I cannot stay. You will do well without me.

I slipped away again into the soft velvet darkness, but this time I was not allowed to stay. I was lifted up in my bed, something was put behind my back, my upper body was positioned higher. It was almost impossible to breathe. I could not endure it, it hurt too much. Everything hurt.

I managed one second at a time. Only one second more. I tried to breathe in. This couldn't work, it was not enough, and anyway, I was dead. What was the good of this? I had lived my life, and it was wonderful and it was horrible. They did not understand, everything was so light on the other side. There was love, an ethereal, indescribable love. And solidarity, a universe of warmth, light and love, a place where I was part of the light and the energy. There I could live and create. Here I was a body, bound in matter and an ocean of pain, worn out and exhausted.

'Mamma, Mamma, come back. I have come to bring you back. It is Tarjei, Tarjei!' Thus spoke the boy with the golden hair.

I saw a face above mine, eyes filled with love. Strong arms were holding me, tears were wetting my face.

Back? I had forgotten my language.

'Tarjei…' I barely managed to whisper his name. 'Yes. I shall come back. I shall manage, for your sake, since you wish it so strongly.'

Tarjei, the boy with the golden hair. I looked at him. There was an aura around his head. I saw in him the sum of all his incarnations and rebirths. Born anew, he was a light on earth.

It was a struggle for Tarjei and for me. He fed me water, drop by drop. He was there all the time and kept me on earth. I was not allowed to go away again. For three days he was awake day and night. He stroked me, healed me, dressed my wounds, washed me. He was there caring for me, talking to me, being with me, and he kept me there. He put a moist cloth on my forehead to cool me down in the choking heat. I could not stand the fan which hung from the ceiling, it was too violent. I felt as if the tiniest breath of air could blow me away from earth again. Then suddenly I remembered the voice. I had agreed to continue my life on earth.

Now I wanted to be there. My son deserved to win his battle, and it really was a battle. When people are in hospital in India, it is the family who takes care of them. He had to do everything all by himself, and still there was no medication, no painkillers. It was a lonely battle for him. He had no one to talk to, I could only whisper a couple of words and everybody else talked Hindi. He phoned Norway every day. When would the air ambulance arrive?

We waited; it was held back, they could not get permission to fly over Pakistan. Three days later the worst of the battle was over. Or was it really over? At least, I was still alive. I did not return to the light. I fought to live, one second at a time. It was almost unbearable, the pain was so overwhelming, so indescribable.

He had sat me up in bed so that no more liquid could get into my lungs. I did not drown. I survived.

I fainted now and then, but it was impossible to sleep. He fell asleep at last, after three days, and slept for a couple of hours on the stone bench beside me. Then it was even worse, and the question came into my mind again. Why am I here? Are there still things for me to do in life? Is it at all possible to get well?

We had to wait a week for the air ambulance, but when at last it came and the helpers appeared clad in their red uniforms, it seemed that even more angels filled the room. I was given painkillers and was carried out into the world by strong arms. The cool air in the plane, the sun and the blue sky outside, the anaesthetist by my side equipped with an analgesic syringe – it was almost like being in heaven again.

At Ulleval Hospital in Norway, I got rest and peace. I got painkillers and medication, but it took a long time. My body was so sick that it was difficult to mend. I became lonely, and the few who were consistently there became even more precious to me.

At times they let in other visitors, but that was too great a strain and I asked them not to. To see them come in, their faces turning white, and watch them fight to keep back the tears, was too hard. I had to comfort them and I had no strength for that. I needed all my strength to survive. It was hard even to talk.

During this time I left my body once again. I tried to share with one of the nurses the joy that I felt over these wonderful experiences, but she became so scared she refused to come back. I was surprised at how much fear and how many barriers still exist among civilised people when it comes to what are called paranormal experiences, but after a while I kept such experiences to myself.

Sometimes I could see through the walls, which appeared to me as a transparent film. This happened one night when the man in the next room died from AIDS. Suddenly it became light and I saw several angels coming to him and taking him away. I was happy for him.

We were both in isolation rooms with double doors out to the corridor. No sound could penetrate and no one had talked to me about him. The morning after his death I told the nurse that it had been a beautiful experience, but she turned pale and went to get the head nurse. She could only confirm what I told her, except for the part about the angels. That was outside her domain.

I suppose there was a defiance in me that made me tell them what I had seen. I became very annoyed by their rigid attitudes, and the way they called my experiences fever fantasies.

Days became weeks and weeks months. I sent thanks to the doctor who came to me one day, sat down on the bed beside me, took my hand and said, 'You must decide to stay here, we cannot manage this ourselves.'

He was right. I wanted to stay on earth because of the others, but the longing for the other side was too strong. I felt myself being pulled towards it. It was unfair to my friends, to my family and the hospital staff to let them strive in vain. I had to manifest my will to stay, to get well.

I found courage in some words I had written in my diary a year earlier:

> *We are not really alive as long as we don't realise that we are going to die and have a relationship with death – understand that we have our time on earth – and that we must use it.*

As I am still here, I must use my time. The time that is left for me in this lifetime.

Yes, life. I'm coming. I shall manage, I shall be totally well again. There are assignments for all of us. Give me time, I am coming back.

I was sent home, and I threw myself wholeheartedly into treatment based on natural remedies. My body was filled to the brim with allopathic medication and it had served its purpose. Now it was necessary to cleanse myself so my body could heal from inside. I was cold, and water seeped out of my body, especially from the legs. Lis, my faithful friend and helper, nursed me and worked relentlessly. She administered foot baths, put me across the bed and put each foot in a bucket.

As the cleansing went on, wounds appeared all over my body. She sprinkled cornflour and powdered clay on them. My mouth swelled up, my lips stood out like a beak covered in sores and scabs. I could neither eat nor speak without my lips cracking open, so again I became silent. Lis listened to my thoughts and gave me water through a straw. It was an awful process, but at the same time it was growth-promoting, and I would not have been without it.

It took three months before I could move carefully about,

then in another couple of months I was at last well again.

This was a real miracle. When I went to see the doctor, he looked at me absent-mindedly and asked for my name.

'That is my journal lying there,' I said and pointed to it. 'I was hospitalised here six months ago.'

He looked at the journal, took a firm hold of his desk, turned around and looked at me unbelievingly. He asked, 'Is this really possible?'

His surprise turned into a smile. Later, when he followed me out into the corridor, he grabbed the head surgeon who was just running by. 'You must stop a minute to say hello to a patient whom you will hardly recognise.'

I was pleased to be an encouragement for them, a reward for their hard work in one of their most difficult wards.

Childhood

It was consciously alive in me, the knowledge of angels, knowing that I was part of something divine. I remembered it all the time, and I was filled with pure smiles and joy until I was two years old. Then rejection and sorrow came into my life. My mother fell seriously ill and had to be sent to a sanatorium. My sister was sent to a summer camp and I was placed in an institution for children. I felt I'd been put away, like a doll nobody needed any longer. I was too young to understand that it was just for a short period, that my father's own despair and the care of two small children was too much for him to handle. There was no one else who could take care of us, and he, of course, had his job to deal with. For a time it seemed he would go down as well. He loved my mother so much that when she went away his spark of life disappeared with her.

Friends and family did their best to tell him that there were two children who needed him. Only three months passed, although to us it felt like an eternity. We were brought home again to a silent house, a home without the song and music we were used to. It was a home with a housekeeper who certainly did not feel any great love for another's woman's children, but who had an eye for my very handsome father.

I had had no visitors during my exile from home. The doctor at the institution told my father that it was better for the children not to see their parents, as there was too much crying when they left again. Without visitors the children were calmer and easier to handle. I can very well believe that now. I became silent and quiet, frozen. Nobody wanted me, nobody loved me. My mother, my father and my sister had given me away. There at the institution they did not love me either. If I was sad, I was beaten. I did not have the right to my life.

My older sister told me later that she remembered the day

they came to fetch me. A small figure stood on the stairs clad in a blue knitted dress and bonnet, totally still as if made of wood – no smile, not a word. I had stopped talking, I no longer smiled.

'You were oozing defiance,' she said.

With hindsight I would have said I was oozing a will to survive, but totally without hope of being recognised or being loved. I had learned that I had to take care of myself, that I was alone.

From the time I was very small I absorbed everything. I listened and I observed. Before I could read I repeatedly asked questions, of my patient, loving father, aunts, uncles, parents of friends and even people on the street. I always found someone to talk to, and I still do. I find people on the street, in shops, on boats, trains and aeroplanes. Suddenly I see a person and know that it is someone I have to talk with, that we have something to give each other, he or she and I, and I have never been rejected.

I can remember them all. I remember the calm old man, sitting on his one-legged stool laying cobblestones in the streets of my youth. I could sit by his side for hours, passing him the next stone, and making him talk. He told me about the valley he came from, about the animals on his parents' farm and his random schooling. He had a grandmother who was clairvoyant and who had even seen the fairies.

I also remember my schoolteacher, Mimi, telling me about her brother who had to escape over the mountain during the war, and who had got his toes so badly frozen that he had to cut them off. She was Jan Baalsrud's sister. My eyes grew big. I was intensely involved, all my senses alert.

I listened with my ears and heart and saw who was sincere and who was talking just to be heard. The worst was when someone told lies; then I felt embarrassed and sad.

My father was a wise and sensitive man who gave me a good rule to live by.

'What is important in life, my child, is the refinement of the heart. Look for that. That is the only thing that counts.' And then, 'Do as you want for yourself, Sisiken, as long as you don't hurt another human being.'

This set me free; he never hindered me.

My grandmother wrote these words from a psalm into my diary: 'The most important thing in the world is not the eagle's flight, but to spread the wings of your heart to shelter others.' This is the upbringing I remember.

There was little fuss and talk about bedtimes. There were only the three of us, my father, my sister and I. At times we had housekeepers, but after a while they fell in love with my father and had to leave. Then for long periods we would go out for dinner again.

I was happy at home when my father was there. He represented security and he was my best friend. When he came home from the office, my world would light up, but the days I spent among friends and at school were rather grey. I was a victim of bullying. I had no mother: I was different.

One day we were playing hopscotch in front of our staircase when Daddy came home from work. He smiled at me and said, 'Today I found the book you wished for, Sisselungen. You can look at it afterwards. We will have dinner in half an hour.'

How I loved him! But how I wished that he would not talk to me like that when the other children were listening. He did not understand what went on outside.

As soon as he had gone inside, they all circled around me and pulled me down the street. 'Sisselungen, I have got the book you wished, for Sisselungen. Daddy's little girl! I have got the book for you.'

I tried to get away, but I was alone and they were many. I turned towards our windows. If Daddy looked out, they would let me go. All I wanted was to be at home, inside where it was safe and with Daddy's warm voice around me.

But I could not see him; there was no one looking out from the window. The children were quick to read my thoughts and one of them said, 'Come, we will show you something. We have got it down at my place. You can take it home and show your father.'

Filled with doubts, I let myself be dragged away. Could it be true? Maybe I was wrong, maybe they really wanted to show me something, something I could bring back to Daddy. We came to the staircase where Tor lived and he opened the door to the cellar. They pushed me in and shut the door.

I was standing there in the dark and for some seconds I did not understand what had happened. They were laughing on the other side of the door.

'Now you can stay there, Daddy's girl! You will be late for dinner, then you will be scolded.'

Darkness – why? Once more I was alone. I was the one who did not belong. How could I be so stupid as to believe that they wanted me to join them? I was not good-looking and clever, and I had no mammy.

Don't be anxious for me, Daddy, I thought. He must not be scared; my poor daddy who was always so good to me.

I just sat there, not even daring to knock on the door. They were sitting on the other side, all those children who had mothers and fathers of their own. I felt doomed for life, and saw myself starving to death, having to stay in the dark for ever.

But I did not cry. Once again I was just the child who had been locked out, the one who was never asked to birthday parties, because we never had parties at our house. Probably, this was the way it had to be.

'What on earth are you doing here?' A man had opened the door and looked sternly at me.

'The other children…'

'Which children? There is nobody here.' He looked at me a bit closer and his voice became gentler. 'Where do you live? It is already dark.'

'I live at the uppermost entrance. It is not far.' I slipped out and ran like a shadow up the street, glancing nervously around me. Fortunately, there were no children to be seen, so I raced home and went into the kitchen.

'But my darling, where have you been? I have been so anxious for you,' said my father. He looked so unhappy that I could not tell him. He was so fond of me. My darling daddy with the sad eyes and the warm voice.

'I forgot about the time. We had such fun.'

My father did not talk much, but he read fairy tales and sang for us in the evening. He was good at reciting and could mimic poets and actors. He read so well that even when I got older, I pretended not to read well enough and asked him to do it.

I curled up on the sofa beside him and imagined the trolls and the princesses, and Hans Christian Andersen's poor boy hidden behind the door listening to the rich little girls talking. If you didn't have the right surname, you couldn't get anywhere in the world.

My heart filled with love for the boy and all the others who were kept away from their heart's desires. Tears often dripped down on our soft, red velour sofa and the cloth hid them. Sometimes Daddy put his hand on my head and scratched my neck gently as I lay there like a little dog, the little dog I wanted so much but never got. I became that little dog, with soft, brown fur and round ears. It looked more like a bear, but it was a dog, and its name was Tass.

One year for Christmas I was given a big toy dog, not brown, but white and hard to the touch. Dutifully I gave it some of my love, and gracefully I christened it Tasselass. I even patted it now and then, often enough for it to become grey and hairless on its back. But I continued to pretend that I was my own little soft, brown dog.

Daddy used to sing, and when he sang it brought tears to my eyes. Other songs made me happy. His dream had been to be an opera singer, and he sang and studied for several years, but when he met my mother, the singing was put aside. That was not how she wanted their life to be. She was a stern lady, my mother, and she wanted him to have a secure employment, and a secure income. My swan of a daddy was swallowed up by the insurance world. He kept his beautiful feathers, but the stars in his eyes lost some of their brilliance. He continued to sing anyway and she played as long as she was well enough. *La Bohème* had been their favourite, and later when Daddy sang 'Your tiny hand is frozen, let me warm it in mine,' my heart would sing and weep at the same time.

Mother died four years later of tuberculosis, just like Mimi in *La Bohème*. My father, my sister and I were the only three left out of our family of four, and the space by the piano was empty. Daddy got rid of it, because it reminded him too much of her.

When did I start to sit on the windowsill at night watching the stars?

By the time I was five, I felt so lonely in my bed it became a black hole. I used to crawl up onto the windowsill and look up towards the stars, longing to be up there, feeling that I belonged there. My true friends, the angels, were up there, and as long as I could sit there and look towards them, I could survive.

My tears often streamed down my cheeks and I licked them. They must not be lost, they were part of me. When sometimes I hurt myself, I licked up the blood too.

Late one evening my father came into my room and found me at the windowsill.

'But my dear child, why are you sitting here?' he asked. He was greatly alarmed, filled not only with love for me, but also with worry and sorrow. 'Why are you crying, my little Sisik?'

It was difficult to answer and I mumbled, 'I was longing so much to be up there.'

He took me back to bed and pulled the duvet around me, tucking me in. 'My little darling, you are icy cold.'

I realised that I was shivering. My thin nightgown did not offer much protection and it was a cold winter's night.

Daddy became very sad, and afterwards he looked in on me more often. I decided for his sake that I had to stop getting up at night. He was mourning my mother, and I had to make him happy.

The child sacrifices herself. This happens again and again. The child believes that if he or she is kind, calm and happy, it will make the grown-ups happy too. This is a disastrous mistake. Adults live in their own worlds and struggle with their own childhoods, their own problems, and their own anxieties.

We all carry our own guilt, our sorrow, and our karma. Lines from a poem by Gunvor Hofmo come to mind: 'Green was the valley of my youth, / No, red – like silent drops of blood.'

'Are you quite sure that I am your child?' I looked seriously at my father, looked into his eyes to find the truth, a secret. There had to be an answer somewhere. I did not really know how to formulate my question, did not even understand what it was that made me uneasy, made everything fit together in such a strange pattern, but these thoughts occupied my mind a lot. I was different; I thought differently from the other children.

My father lifted his eyes from the book he was reading and

looked at me a bit absent-mindedly. Then he patted my head gently and assured me, 'Yes, my baby, that is absolutely certain.' He nodded as if to underline what he had said, but I was not entirely convinced.

One day when I was a little girl I was sitting in front of the radio, drawing, and suddenly the most heavenly song floated into the room. In a way it seemed familiar, but it did really not belong there.

I sat there mesmerised, listening, and suddenly I felt very happy. When the last note died away I fell down and cried myself into and through a deep longing to be back in that place where they sang so beautifully. That was where I belonged, of that I was certain, but at the same time I belonged here with Daddy. This made me very confused and sad. There was something I so much wanted to understand, but I could not ask, I did not know how. It helped to feel Daddy's hand on my neck. He did not say much – he seldom did – but it felt safe to have him there and I was glad that he did not speak.

The song on the radio had been from a Russian Orthodox choir. Reincarnation? Had I been born anew? Who talked about reincarnation in the thirties in Norway? Now it is almost acceptable, in some circles at least, but during my growing-up years I was sometimes asked, 'Are you really Norwegian?' I wanted to answer 'No,' because within me I felt this was true.

Our Sunday walks, which were a great joy to me, also became a time for discussion between us. I wanted to go to Sunday school – I felt a pull towards the church – but my father was less enthusiastic about it. He had been brought up in an atmosphere of Christianity that was too stern. So sometimes I went to Sunday school first and then we went for a late walk; at other times we went walking early. His love of nature helped to form me, as did the talks we had when we walked in the woods and the mountains.

In church I was faced again with the world's injustice. The other children got golden stars in their book, but I did not, as I was not there often enough. I lost faith in the Sunday school teacher.

Some of the joy I felt in going there also disappeared. We little ones had to sit in a corner of the church, while the bigger children sat just in front of the altar, where I felt that I belonged. God and Jesus wanted me to sit there, I felt sure about that. I felt that I was God's child, and that there was no difference between us, the small ones, and the big ones. Sunday school was strange, so was the church, and people were not at all as nice and as cheerful as I expected. I wondered about it, and the wondering brought me closer to myself, but I was not able to explain why. I remembered something distant and good, love and solidarity. My life should be a path walked in pain, joy and wonder.

Big and small helpers

My mother's sister, who took care of us a lot, gave me back my belief in love in this world. When she had said prayers with me in the evening, she kissed my cheek and said, 'God bless you, my child.' It warmed my heart and brought tears into my eyes. That's the way it was. I was blessed, never alone. That is what I believed, hoped and wanted deep inside.

My sister and I went to live with my aunt each summer. We were put on a boat called *Oscarsborg* with our wicker trunk and carpet bag, and went off by sea to Soon. It was good to be there. It was a wonderful, old house with lots of paintings on the walls. There were a grand piano, a cello and a guitar, and there was a big garden with bushes and trees and many hiding places. It was a dream place for children. My aunt was mild and kind but my uncle was very stern, and I was rather afraid of him. He did not care much for children and we were told to be quiet when he was reading. He never talked to me, not until I was sixteen years old, but he played the piano and the cello and it made my heart dance.

I lived and was intensely aware of life when there were no people around me, in the manner of most children without television or other entertainments to disturb them. I listened to the grasshoppers and sang with them at night in my bed in auntie's house. It was a very old house, almost three hundred years, and it was alive, creaking and heaving. My bedroom was just beside my uncle's studio and the air was filled with exciting, wonderful scents of old timber and turpentine from his paintings.

I hoped and expected that ghosts would appear, but unfortunately it never happened.

For my comfort I had found a small knothole in the panelled wall over my bed. I peeped into the dark behind it and imagined trolls and fairies.

Sometimes I hung out of the window and talked to the grasshoppers. The summer nights were light and lonely, and it was a long way down from the loft in the big house to the other rooms on the ground floor.

My uncle often sat down there and played. It was wonderful, and sometimes I sneaked down the steep, dark staircase and sat behind the door listening to the music, the laughter and the conversation. If I was discovered, I was scolded, sent up to my room again and told to go to sleep.

Sleep? That was not possible with the grasshoppers singing outside. There must have been thousands of them. Were grass-hoppers happy? They sounded lonely, even in their thousands.

Loneliness... yes. Isn't childhood always a lonely condition? We all have a room inside ourselves where we are alone, where we let nobody in, a room we can and should fill with ourselves and with everything that is ours. We are the sum of many lives, of that I am certain. We are all born again, and in childhood and youth we are supposed to get our experiences in order before we start our current life. All children have the ability to do this if they are left alone to inquiry and reflection, without adults intervening to talk, govern, control and educate them. That need to educate often comes from their own insecurities, and the more we as grown-ups are present in ourselves, the easier it is for us to help our children build their own foundations, find their own security and become self-confident.

I loved the sea and wanted to bathe all the time, but my aunt was anxious and watched me too carefully. When Daddy was there he gave me more freedom and I could play in the sea all the time. I had not yet learned to swim but I walked out until the water reached my shoulders and I stood there, watching the children jumping off the raft into the deep water. Then they crawled back up, jumped off and came up again. Just wait, I thought. I'll soon be able to do that. Then I lost my balance, went under and sat on the sandy bottom. There was a rushing around me – this was another world. Was this really what being a fish was like? It was so beautiful I gasped, and swallowed water. It was lovely.

In the short moment before Daddy came and pulled me up again, I had the time to experience another dimension. It became quite light, and I saw pictures, colours and heard music from afar. I was not at all scared, I was mesmerised and I knew that I was part of it all. I was about four years old, and for the first time in this life I was in another dimension.

After I was rescued I wanted to share my experience with my father, but he was preoccupied with the fact that I had nearly drowned. He wouldn't listen, so I said nothing more. There were always so many exciting things happening around me.

I could never stand seeing anybody unfairly treated, teased or tormented. I hated it most when it happened to animals, because they could not defend themselves. I still have memories of seeing the cruelty of children to animals, and of the indifference of grown-ups who did not have the will to prevent it. One day I was on my way back from school with a friend, and at the churchyard wall we were surrounded by boys. They were screaming and laughing. 'Come and see what we have made!' they cried. And there, just inside the gate, they had built a little town with houses and roads. On the roads crawled two little birds. The boys had cut their wings off and the poor things were crawling along, covered in blood and sand. A red mist formed over my eyes.

'No, no, no!' I cried. I ran out into the street and stopped the first person who came along. I caught hold of his coat, told him what had happened and asked him to come and help.

'That is the way of boys,' he said, and he pulled himself loose and went away, without so much as a glance through the gate.

That was the moment when I lost the rest of my faith in my fellow man.

I cried for days and weeks because of those little birds and because other people did not prevent such things from happening. I sought refuge in my father and sat close to him when he came back from the office.

'That man was afraid,' he said. 'Many grown-ups are afraid and do not dare to interfere in anything. They don't feel safe in themselves.' He patted my head and put his hand on my neck and left it there. 'I think those little birds are dead now, and in heaven they will get new wings,' he said.

I knew that, of course, but what about all the other cruelties in the world? Many dark events churned around in my mind.

'We can only do as best we can ourselves,' Daddy said. 'Then the world will be a bit better to live in.' He sang for me and I felt uplifted.

As a child, I begged and begged to have an animal, a cat, a dog or even a mouse, but Daddy was adamant there would be no animals in our flat. I could just forget about that. Animals were not meant to live in towns; they belonged in the country.

I tried to deceive him. I knew of a kitten that was about to be given away. My sister went along with the plot, promising not to tell Daddy, and I would hide the kitten in our room when he was home. It went well for about a week but then the kitten got out of the window while I was asleep, walked along the cornice to our neighbour's window and paid her a visit. She rang the doorbell while we were at breakfast.

'I have just come to give Sissel her cat back,' she said. 'It has been on a little visit to me.' My father's expression was priceless.

'Sissel has no cat,' he said rather stiffly, and closed the door. He did not like to be disturbed, especially not by our female neighbours. My sister's face was red with the effort of keeping her laughter back, and she bent low over her porridge. Daddy started to suspect mischief and looked at me more closely.

'It can't be you?'

'Oh, Daddy, please. I just got it.'

But he said, 'No cat here. You knew that!'

I was not easily stopped. I tried again, this time with hamsters. They lived in a cage, at least while he was home, and they could not escape. I hid the cage in my open cupboard and hung up a curtain in front of it.

It went well for a fortnight, then one evening my father came into my room as the hamsters were scratching and gnawing to their hearts' content. I tried to make as much noise as possible but to no avail. The scratching was too strong.

'What on earth are you up to now?'

When he was told, he just shook his head. But they had to go the next day. So after that I had to get my enjoyment from the animals I managed to meet outside of the house.

I went to all the exhibitions of cats and dogs, and I rode horses and talked to them whenever I had the opportunity.

One day I was at an exhibition standing outside a cage with a big dog inside. The dog had called to me.

'Why don't you take him out of his cage?' I asked the owner, who stood nearby.

'He is a watchdog,' he answered. 'He would bite the leg of the first person who came by.'

'He is unhappy and lonely,' I said and looked at him defiantly. He just turned on his heel and went away. I sat down on my heels and looked down on the floor and talked to my friend in the cage. I spoke to him for a long time in a low, calm voice. After a while I opened the door of the cage and went in, and when the man came back I was sitting in the cage with my arms around the dog. Its head rested on mine and we just sat there together and were happy. Time had stopped. The man said nothing more.

When the exhibition closed, he surprised me. 'I would never have believed that,' he said.

Suddenly he was speaking to me like an equal, and that encouraged me. I looked at him and asked, 'Couldn't you pat him now?'

He did not answer that, as he was too occupied in putting the cage onto his van. He just grunted by way of a farewell and disappeared. I was sad to see my new friend leave Frogner Stadium in the back of his owner's van.

Why is it so good for children to be with animals? Because they are natural, they just exist. They don't play roles as people do. They are our connection to nature. They can be intimate without being anxious, shy or withdrawn. We can be with them and just exist, as we can with very small children before the world destroys them.

Modern, civilised man has forgotten this, forgotten how to exist within himself. We have to relearn it. We must find the way back to ourselves, to what we are in our innermost selves, our inner universe, where man is never alone.

Since I was a little girl animals have always come to me. Like the Indians, I went out into the woods early in the morning, getting close to the birds, hares, foxes and elk. I was part of nature and I communicated with them in silence. Telepathic communication, it was called, I later learned. I fed field mice in the garden and in the shed. They ate sausage, bread and sardines out of my hand and I sent my thoughts to them.

'I am your friend. I am very happy that you are here. The world becomes nicer when you are here.' I am certain that they answered me.

My aunt and uncle in Soon had a dog called Binna. She was old and preferred to lie in a sunbeam on the floor and sleep, but she had soft fur and nice round ears that I could lift and tell secrets to.

Binna was very patient and kind; she would let me put my arms around her and use her as a pillow as long as I shared my cakes with her. This lasted two years and then she was gone.

'She had become too old,' my aunt told me. 'And now she is gone.'

I thought a lot about this. There was something they weren't telling me, but I didn't find out any more about it. I asked my uncle, but he gave even fewer answers. He just gave a grunt.

We children were disturbing him. He accepted the sight of us, but he did not want to hear us. The house seemed very empty without Binna, but fortunately there were other animals around that I could talk to.

One day a squirrel arrived. Suddenly it was sitting in the open door to the living room, looking at me. It got tamer every day, coming especially when I was alone, and as time passed it became a daily visitor at lunchtime. It stole nuts from my plate and butter from the pot, and I gave it water in its own little saucer. At times it came onto my lap when I was alone in the garden, and it did not move even if I stroked its back with my fingers.

One day it stole a little chocolate from me. That was not meant to happen. I had kept the chocolate for so long, and was looking forward to eating it myself in peace and quiet under my favourite tree in the garden. I ran after the squirrel to get my chocolate back, but it was too quick. In no time it was up in a tree and sat there, very pleased, opening up its loot and letting the paper fall down on my head. It ate all the chocolate and got rather ill, lying there without moving, stretched out on the branch with its paws hanging down. Some hours later it tried to open an eyelid when I called it, but quickly fell asleep again.

It managed to survive the chocolate, but did not survive a gunshot. One day I found it lying dead in the garden. For me this was a new meeting with death, a death that seemed quite meaningless.

During the following years many animals came to me and stayed with me for shorter or longer periods. Tjorven came in a very special way that I can only call God's will.

A friend of mine lost her little dog and cried inconsolably on the phone.

'You must find another,' I told her. 'Go and find one at the Association of the Relocation of Animals. Then you will do a good deed at the same time. You will give love to a little creature which needs you.'

It was decided that I should investigate for her, so I called, and got a heartfelt welcome. I was given the phone number of a man who needed to find a new owner for his mother's little dog. His mother was old and about to go into hospital, and she had no hope of being able to keep the dog. She was already having difficulty walking it.

This led to many phone calls, as my friend did not want a male dog, and certainly not a mongrel.

'No, you'll just have to call and say no thanks,' she told me.

Say 'no thanks'? As so often before, I thought, Sissel, why do you always have to help everyone and fix everything? Now it will only be sadder for everyone and that was not the idea… Or was it?

I called and said I was sorry, but we could not take the dog. He begged me. 'But why can't you take it? You have such a kind voice and nobody else wants it. I don't know what to do. I have a big Alsatian dog; it doesn't like Tjorven, it will bite his head off.'

'I cannot help you. We only have a small flat, and I have a husband, a child and a big dog already.'

Even so, I promised I would sleep on it. I went to bed early and said my prayer: 'Lord, if I am supposed to have this dog, please give me a sign.'

I slept and in the morning I did not remember dreaming, so I asked the question again in my morning prayer. 'If I am meant to help Tjorven, let me meet him on my way to work today.'

I did not know where the little dog lived, except that it was somewhere in the same city, Oslo. I left home early on my bicycle, due to start work at seven, but allowing myself an extra half-hour in case God wanted to show me something. It was Sunday morning and the streets were deserted as I bicycled around, up one street and down the next. There was nobody to be seen. Well, it was maybe too much to expect that I should get an answer in this way.

But no, it couldn't be true! My heart began to beat faster as far ahead down the street I saw an elderly lady walking a little dog on a lead. I sent a quick glance to the heavens. 'Is this a joke?' I said. 'Is it possible? Well, at least I'll do my bit!' I jumped off my bike and went to meet them, bent down and said, 'What a sweet dog!'

This was not entirely true. The little dog was extremely unat-tractive and snarled at me threateningly. His open mouth showed a row of decayed teeth, and one of his ears stood up while the other dropped down. His coat seemed sparse and he was a sad sight as he watched me suspiciously through red-rimmed eyes. My heart filled with sympathy and concern. Could this little skinny animal be…? 'What is your name, then?' I asked and patted his back.

'Tjorven,' said the lady.

I could write a lot about Tjorven, but it won't be here and now. I loved him dearly and we had three good years together.

Outside the trodden path of sight

When did I start to see things before they happened? I don't know – I never really thought about it. I suppose I thought that it was normal, that we all saw what was still to come and acted accordingly. I often sent letters or flowers or went to visit friends when I felt that something was wrong, when I sensed that they had difficulties and were struggling to handle them on their own, or when I knew that they were about to leave for the other side. I was surprised when a friend became very alarmed and told me, 'No, Sissel, you must not say things like that!'

A friend had just left and I said, 'That was the last time we will see her.'

I stood deep in thought, wondering if there was anything we could do, and when my friend reacted like that I explained what I had sensed and asked him to share his own feelings with me, but he refused to discuss it. I discovered that most people were reluctant to talk about death. Our friend died one month later. And after this episode I became more careful about what I said.

It is not easy to know how to handle our foresight of what is about to happen. Are we supposed to warn others, or should we simply try to ease a person's last moments? I have come to believe that the latter choice is the right one. I know of few people who have been able to use such knowledge positively. I completely stopped talking about future events after a very bad experience with a friend. She had a bad relationship with her mother, and was very bitter about incidents in her childhood. As the years passed she came to hate her mother and held her responsible for her own difficult life situation. One day, after we had had a long and intimate conversation, I suggested she should speak to her mother in the same way as she had spoken to me. I asked her to talk about herself and her feelings, and at the same time try to see her mother as a little child with her own sorrows and difficulties. 'You do not have much time left to put this in order,' said I. 'Your mother is going to die within two or three months.' My friend was furious and a whole year went by before I saw her again.

Her mother did die, three months after our conversation, without the two of them talking things over. I didn't know her mother. They lived far away and there was nothing I could have done to help them. It would have been better not to say anything.

To think of our fellow human beings and to send them light and love has to be the best help we can give.

I also had a foreboding when my own brother-in-law was about to leave for the other side.

What do we do, what *can* we do? I did not know the time, the place or how he would die, I only knew that his time had come.

My sister and brother-in-law have always been close to me.

I have lived with them for long periods more than once. In a way we were parents for each other's children, and my brother-in-law was like a brother to me, even if I never mentioned it. He was a man of few words and we had never spoken much. Most of the time the two of them lived abroad, but they decided to move back to Norway when he retired, and a couple of weeks before they arrived I had an irresistible urge to write to him. I told him that I had always thought of him as a brother, the brother I had always wanted, that I was fond of him and was looking forward to their coming home. The day before their arrival, I phoned their neighbour here in Norway and asked her to buy flowers and put them in front of their door. I also wrote them a warm letter of welcome.

My sister called and thanked me. My brother-in-law had been very touched by the letter and the flowers, and I was invited to come for a visit. It was not a convenient time, because I was leaving for Copenhagen two days later on a job and had a lot to do, but my feelings and intuition told me to go at once. I took my camera, bought two films, jumped into my car and went there straight away.

The three of us had two lovely days together. We worked in the garden, laughed and talked more easily than ever before, and I took a series of photographs of them. Then I had to leave. When I drove up the driveway and out on the road, I turned and waved. I knew that it was the last time I would see him, and I drove back to Oslo with tears streaming from my eyes.

He was killed in a car accident a few days later. I was driving along the motorway on my way back from Copenhagen when suddenly I saw a sparkling light. I saw, heard and felt him. I cried out his name and knew that he had gone from us for the time being. Other tasks awaited him.

We can only live out the best in ourselves. I think that is what it is all about while we are here on earth. To exist fully, to live in joy and solidarity as if every day were the last one. Death leads into the next life, it is a birth into the 'bardo condition', which is the life between our lives here on earth. It is only painful for the ones left behind on earth. We do not want to lose each other, we cannot bear the notion that the ones we love should leave us; but for those who die, death is release. They have finished their task here and gone on to the next one.

When we have finished our life here on earth, we leave the physical body, just as we change our clothes when they are worn out. We each leave our bodies, and after some time on the other side we come back in a new body for a new existence.

I thought it was horrible when my own father died. I lost my best friend. I could talk to him about everything; he was a wise man and knew how to listen. Now he was going, and I was left. I stood there holding his hand, stroking his high forehead.

'Thank you, Daddy, for all you have given me.'

I kissed his forehead and saw that he had attained sublime peace. I knew he had gone into the divine light and love on the other side of life.

I could not help mourning my loss, but I also felt joy that he was well. In a way he was still with me through all the stories and memories he had shared, all he had been to me. 'Do not mourn his death,' a good friend told me. 'Enjoy the fact that he has lived.'

I prayed a lot during that time. I prayed to have a child, a child to whom I could give love and friendship and with whom I could share Daddy's stories and fairy tales. I prayed that I might attract an old soul, a soul I already knew, a soul who could meet me in a mutual wish to learn and experience and walk the way together. I prayed morning and night, and might sometimes have been absent-minded at work. I worked as a silversmith and had wonderful freedom, and I slid into prayer while I sat there with my jewellery. Three months later my son announced his presence. I knew the moment he was conceived; it was like a light coming in and it touched me like the wing of a butterfly. I couldn't sleep. I got out of bed and I thanked God. I went out in the park and watched the stars. I talked with the angels up above, and I laughed with joy.

I didn't walk downtown to work, I danced. I hopped over the kerbstones like a little girl playing hopscotch: *don't tread on the lines…*

I arrived too early at work that day. There was nobody there but I had all the time in the world and I had already started to get to know my son. He had come back to earth and we were to continue our work together.

Later, when I went to see the doctor, he said. 'No, you are not pregnant.' I just laughed and said that I knew better.

Yes, we all mourn when we are left behind, it takes time to let go of the people we love, but we have to realise that we keep the dead back with our sorrow. We hinder them from going on, make them stay around us instead of going on into the light where they are expected, and where they are meant to continue their own growth.

We can even hold people back from leaving their bodies, and we should be careful about that. How can we know what they really want? Is it the higher will of the dying person to go over to the other side now, or do they really want to live longer in this world?

We have to be aware of this when we pray for the families of friends who are sick.

We may pray for the patient to be held in the light, pray that he gets in contact with his higher will, pray that he meets with his own angel; but we must not pray for his recovery. The sick person himself must ask for that and wish for it. If a relative asks me to send healing, I must add to the prayer, 'Lord, thy will be done.'

We might also address the sick person's soul and ask that his or her higher will be done. We must learn to accept that we don't always know what is best. The will of a person's soul or higher self will always agree with God's will, but on the personal level the conscious awareness may seem, and often is, rather confused.

One day I was asked by a distressed grandmother to send healing to her newborn grandchild, who was born with a heart defect. The baby was very weak and the doctors did not want to operate on her.

This was difficult for me. I could not know this little girl's higher will, but I knew that she was very much a wanted child and that her parents and grandparents were devastated by her frailty.

For two days I sent healing and I prayed for her, but the situation was unchanged.

The third day the little child appeared before me while I meditated. She looked five times bigger than a normal newborn baby, but that was how they usually appeared to me when they die.

'You must let me go,' she said. 'I want to go back, but I will come to them again in a couple of years.'

I phoned her grandmother and told her what had happened, and explained that I had to do what I had been told. The news that the child would come back was a bright spot in the middle of the sorrow.

I went to my altar and prayed that the child's higher will should be done, and she died that day.

During the time that followed, I kept in contact with the family and they experienced a rich spiritual growth and progress. When we learn to accept what is to be, we grow. Three years later, the child was born again. Often we incarnate ourselves to stay only for a short while, sometimes to have a particular experience ourselves, at other times so that our parents will learn and progress. There is no death.

As human beings we lose the gift of seeing totally. We know

everything, but after just a short time here on earth we forget. If we were able to remember everything, we would not be able to learn, and we would not have to put any effort into the solving of problems.

It is terrible for us to lose those we love when we are unable to see clearly, and when we don't remember that we will meet again and again.

Our thoughts have enormous power. To put it another way, we as human beings have enormous powers. We have power enough for just about anything, but what we lack is trust and faith.

We came from God, and we were created by God at the beginning of time. We are part of God, and we are divine beings, so why shouldn't we have divine abilities and powers?

Of course we have, and we are meant to use them.

Once I read an almost incredible story about a mother whose prayers saved her son from death. It was a well-documented story and it touched me deeply.

Later I had many experiences of helping my own son by praying for him. Each time it happened, I had a premonition of danger, and when I see danger and at the same time get a warning message, I take it as a sign that I am meant to help.

One day I was sitting working on a piece of jewellery and concentrating very hard, when suddenly I saw my son's face clearly before me. At the same time I had a strong feeling of danger. I knelt down by my altar and I saw and heard a car driving at high speed, then the sound of broken glass and a child screaming. I recognised the narrow, twisting road my son was driving along, and saw the landscape around him. I shouted, 'Lord, lift him out of this!' And at the same time I thanked Him for hearing my prayer.

At once I was filled with peace and I was surrounded by light. I looked at the clock and went back to my work feeling quite at ease.

Half an hour later, the phone rang. It was my son.

'You must not be afraid,' he said, 'but I have been stopped by the police. I am not allowed to drive on.'

'That is a case of a heard prayer, Tarjei,' I said.

There was a moment of quiet. 'I think you are right.' he said.

'I'll phone you tonight.' I knew he was deeply moved.

Later we talked for a long time. I told him what I had seen, describing the landscape and the twisting road. Everything was as it had been. He had been driving very fast, feeling depressed and taking a chance with his life, then quite suddenly he had calmed down and reduced his speed. The car was filled with song, and he told me he felt a presence hard to describe. It had filled him with awe and joy and made him want to sing.

Behind the next bend, the police were waiting. My son lost his licence, and therefore his job. He had to go to jail, where he discovered his gift for giving light and healing, and this totally changed the direction of his education.

He gave his guardian angels a lot of work, and I had many opportunities to send him help, but that is another story. Each time he was in trouble I received a warning and was able to see him and sense where he was.

Before each of us incarnated into this life, we knew that we should take our parts in creating a better world for everybody to live in. We should work to promote light and love. This was the road we decided to walk while we were still on the other side, before we were born anew. But many of us had such a painful start in life that we closed off and forgot our own message. Just to survive became challenge enough, and we fell into the same trap as we had in so many former lives; we completely forgot to live, and did nothing more than exist. This is not right. We are supposed to enjoy life. Do not believe what the old Pietists preach.

We should not bend our heads down in shame and pray, but should lift our heads in joy and be thankful. Thankfulness is the only prayer.

We are not told by our guide, master, angel, and God to live in meekness and asceticism, but to live with every fibre in our bodies, to be thankful for our lives and pray that our angels will always be with us.

Enjoy your home with all its beautiful things, your bicycle, your car and the good food you eat; but do not live for these things.

Don't waste your time weeping for all those who suffer; that will help nobody. Those you are meant to help will come to you in person or by letter and ask for your help.

In the old days the maxim was give a tenth of what you earn to those in need. This is still valid today. It is mentioned in the Bible, but seems to be forgotten and have little value now. The richer we become, the greater our need to buy and own even more. Many people have lost the ability to see and to help others.

This may be because they are afraid to get involved. It could bring me difficulties, even unpleasantness, they rationalise. But, why not turn these thoughts around? We create our own society; we create our own day. What we all really want is an open and friendly society. Be aware, be present, and notice those who come your way.

Is there something you should learn from them, or are you meant to give them your help? We have come into this life of our own free will in order to experience and to solve problems. We are here to learn, to work on our own development and to help others with theirs. Together we are responsible for saving the earth. We must stop squandering the gifts the earth has given us, and we must stop exploiting each other. Everything we do to others, we do to ourselves, and everything we give to each other, we give to ourselves. We are all cells in the huge body of the earth, dependent on each other, and each and every one of us is indispensable. We are all one. We are all equally necessary for the whole, and the sooner we understand this, the better. If we believe that we can close our eyes and forget all that is happening around us, we are seriously mistaken. Everything affects us as if it has happened to each of us.

Life is filled with new tasks every day, adjusted to the ability each of us has to tackle them.

Each time we think, This is too much for me, we let our own anxiety and our own judgement gain the upper hand.

'As your days are, so shall your strength be.' This is what we have been promised and that is how it is!

Breathe! Breathe in deeply, and take in your fill of faith and trust.

You are, I am, we are…

We are power, love and light.

If we do not realise that we are divine beings with enough strength to create our own world, we will have betrayed ourselves. But this demands something of you. It demands that you actively take a serious look at yourself. Then it will give you joy, and you will feel stronger every day you live according to your own will, your real will, the will of your higher self. Follow the road you have chosen, solve your chosen task.

It might take a while to find it because our life is filled with so many unessential things. We let ourselves be influenced by the overwhelming materialism of our society.

The time has come to inwardly trust yourself, listen deep inside yourself and find the way to your treasures. Rich, deep joy lies forgotten and hidden inside, behind the insecurity and anxiety. Along with this joy is your primordial power which gives you the ability to meet what lies ahead of you. There is certainly no reason to bow your head.

When we find the path that is right for us, we feel relief. The soul is overjoyed. This spreads over onto the personality. Everything is as it is supposed to be. This is the meaning of life.

Everything is sacred. We could learn a lot from the old Indians. They understood that the earth, animals and people are dependent on each other and belong together.

Every thought we think will affect those around us and the whole universe. Before we understand this, we wander around, confused, caught up in our own difficulties and struggles.

We have responsibility for every thought and word we create. When we understand this properly we will begin to create good thoughts. Then your world will also be better.

Healing – everybody can do it

What is it other than healing when a mother strokes her sick child, or when we pat and cuddle a crying child who has been hurt? We often touch each other in order to soothe each other's pains. We want to ascertain that we are there for each other, that we are with the sufferer in their illness or sorrow. We do not think of the force which is there within us; but it is there, our ability is there, and we can train it by consciously using it.

Put your hands on your partner, your child, your friends. Stroke a bad back, put your hands on a stiff neck, and at the same time concentrate, breathe in and fill yourself with light and energy from the universe. Feel that you are receiving power all the time, that you constantly recharge your own batteries and at the same time act as a channel for higher powers.

With practice, you will focus your ability to heal, to restore health. Get into the habit of putting your hands on friends and family and at the same time, focus your mind on wishing everything that is good for them. With practice, you will get a better contact. We don't touch each other enough in our society.

One day in Bogstadveien, Oslo, I helped an elderly lady across the street. She had been standing there for some time and had started to cross a couple of times, but had changed her mind. I was buying vegetables at a stand on the other side and had watched her. I went over to her, put my arm around her and asked if we should cross the street together. She started to cry and took hold of my wrist to make sure that I was real and would not disappear at once. She told me that for many years nobody had held her.

Another time in town I saw an elderly gentleman in the middle of the street. He was standing there waving his arms, visibly asking for help, and nobody was reacting. Some people were even laughing at him, as if he were some sort of entertainment.

I marched out into the street, stopped the traffic and helped him onto the pavement. We stood there for a while talking, and he did not cry but his voice quivered as he complained that the traffic was getting heavier and heavier. When he had been a little boy they had been able to go sledding in the street and there were more horses than cars, but now it was difficult to cross the street quickly enough.

I'll spare my readers any more stories like these, but I could fill pages with them. They are about healing too. Everything we do out of love for our fellow human beings is a form of healing. Our actions give nourishment, acknowledge their inner child, offer love for the loneliness within them.

If you want to actively start healing somebody, the first thing you have to do is to cleanse their aura. The aura is the invisible ether body which surrounds us all. It is like the physical body and surrounds you, extending about two centimetres outside the skin. In addition, we each have an astral body and a mental body outside this. Some people have auras stretching far out from their physical bodies, sometimes for several metres.

You should always have one or several burning candles in the room so that you can throw away what you pull out. Also, put out a bowl with clear water to serve the same purpose, to gather up negative matter. You can also rinse your hands there when you feel that you have something from the patient that you have to get rid of.

It is preferable to let the patient lie down, and this is more pleasant for them than sitting up. Put your hands at right angles to his or her body, about twenty centimetres away, then stroke from the head towards the feet and beyond. Repeat this four or five times. You will stroke away the bad things in the aura, before you start healing the body itself, and a sensitive person will feel this almost as strongly as when you actually touch their body.

Sometimes you may feel that you should hold your hands further away from the body, that something bad is sitting further out, and that you have to stroke it away first. The negative things sitting in the aura will reach the body later and become pains or sickness. Everything is psychosomatic. No sickness or pain is merely physical.

When you have cleansed the aura, put your hands on the sore or painful spot.

You will often feel your hands getting very warm, but if they don't it does not matter. The important thing is that you are conscious of what you are doing, that you wish to be a channel. You are there to help your friend get rid of the sickness or the pains.

Hold your hands on the sore spot for five to twenty minutes. Afterwards you can hold your hands about fifteen to twenty centimetres from the body and send light and power, healing from a distance. This will continue to be effective for a longer period.

It is important that you receive all the time, that you use the force from the universe. Let the force flow through you and into the spot you want to heal.

I have forgotten this several times. I used too much of my own life force and therefore fell seriously ill. This happened not only in India, but also another time when I felt it very dramatically. I was on my way home after having been to heal a sick, elderly lady. I was driving on the motorway, but in my thoughts I was still with her. I was thinking that she was old and weak and I was young and strong.

'Lord, let me take her pain, so that she can be well,' I prayed.

It happened: as soon as I had thought the words, I slumped over the steering wheel in pain and almost drove off the road. We must know and remember that we are not here to take over other people's pains. Everybody has their own karma which they are supposed to live out themselves, but we can help each other. We can pass on light, love and energy from the universe, but we are not supposed to give our own life force away. A person can give so much to other people that he becomes totally worn out.

This often happens in relationships. One person gives, the other absorbs energy without either of them realising it. I often recommend separate bedrooms, or at least that the beds are spaced wide apart, because you lie beside your partner every night for six to nine hours. One person is reloading the batteries while the other gets up deadly tired, and nobody understands why.

This is, of course, not always the case. If both parties are present in themselves and have open communication, they will both be able to take in energy, or prana. Both will be able to recharge their batteries and feel refreshed and fit after a good night's sleep.

Funnily enough, this also happens when people are newly in love. Both are open, and it is a wonderful thing as long as it lasts, because both are able to give, and both are open to the energy flowing into them from outside.

Prana is a word from Sanskrit that means absolute energy. Besides oxygen, it is prana that fills us when we breathe in deeply and fully.

Visualise a beam of light from the universe, from God, that goes into your heart and to the crown chakra, a point on top of your head. Feel the force that fills you. This is the life force, the universal life force mirroring your own.

Preferably, you should do this every time you breathe in, but this is too much to ask. I know of no ordinary human being who does it. I once asked a guru about this and he told me that only the great masters can do it. But do your best anyway. Do it consciously when you remember it and every time you do healing work.

When you have finished healing, you must rinse your arms and hands in cold water. You can also put some cold water on your neck and on your crown chakra. If your patient is very sick, it is a good idea to take a cold shower afterwards to rid yourself of what you may have taken on.

Learn to protect yourself by pulling golden rings around you.

Imagine that you are inside a golden egg which protects you from everything negative from outside. It helps to move your hand in big circles in front of you. Pass your hand down your right side and over to the left below the pelvis, then up the left side and to the right over the head. Do this seven times, all the time keeping your hand as far from the body as you can. You should do this several times a day if you are very sensitive; it can spare you from much unpleasantness and from feeling tired. It is essential to do it before working with a client, and the same method can be used to protect your own house. Imagine that you pull golden rings around your house when you leave it to go to school or to work.

If you are very sensitive, pulling golden rings around you can be useful to protect yourself again and again when you go to places where many people are gathered, or if you feel that someone is pulling energy from you. It is not necessary to do it in front of them, of course.

We must get used to always being conscious of what is going on inside us.

This means that you should always be present in yourself, and have the centre of gravity in hara, which is the next lowest chakra, just below the navel.

We have seven main chakras; the crown chakra on top of the head; the third eye chakra on the forehead between and a little above the eyes; the throat chakra; the heart chakra in the middle of the breast; the solar plexus chakra at the diaphragm, right under the ribs; the hara chakra just below the navel; and the root chakra, down below between the anus and the genitals. These are wheels of energy, and in healthy, vital people they turn around constantly. When there is sickness or old age, they will often turn slower and slower.

Concentrate your attention on the hara now. Feel that you are present there. Visualise that your consciousness is in your belly, in hara. It is easier to concentrate on what you are doing, when you have your gravity point in hara. Also, we do not so easily lose our tempers or lose balance when we are present in hara.

Exercises in earthing are also useful. You can read more about that in the chapter about meditation. It often happens that we give without being conscious of it, and therefore it is important that we protect ourselves, and remember to draw rings around ourselves even when we are comfortable with the company we are in. This is easily forgotten, especially when we are enjoying ourselves with pleasant people. I am a good example of this myself.

My sister and I were in England on a course in overtone singing. There were about forty of us together at a lovely place called Hazelwood. It was an old mansion with beautiful old stone buildings, and the sessions took place in the estate's old stone church.

We were chanting, which is to say that we were doing overtone singing and voice exercises all day. It was a very powerful experience for many of us. There were strong feelings and lots of tears right from the first day, and we had long talks in our groups in the evenings. I love singing, and I very much enjoyed being with all these people. I was open and very excited by what we were doing, and the idea of protecting myself and earthing myself was far from my mind.

On the second day I felt pain in my body, and my back became stiff and locked. I did not give myself the time to find out where it came from; I thought it might be because of a water line running under the house. Such water lines can send out a radiation which is harmful to health, and can cause pains in the body. I changed house and bed, but this did not help: the pain got worse, and on the third day I was taken to an osteopath in the nearby village. He was very interested by my work as a healer, and I thought he asked rather a lot of questions about my working methods.

The treatment made me a bit better and I managed to walk down the steps and into the car by myself. But back at Hazelwood my back stiffened again, and the next morning I was just as ill. I had to be carried down to the church, where I lay on my back, taking part in the course, both that day and the next. It felt as if knives were cutting into my back and after a while I was completely helpless. Again I was taken down to the osteopath, and this time he only looked at me without making any moves to start treatment. He asked more seriously about my experiences as a healer and I told him about the time when I was very ill in India. After that he treated me, but it did not help much. My body ached; just to be touched was painful, and after the treatment he sat down, took my hands and spoke to me urgently.

'You must leave here as soon as possible. You are taking on the sorrow and suffering from the others. You are enclosed in a narrow valley, in a house of stone. It is too late to protect yourself, and there is no other possible way of getting rid of these pains. Go at once, leave today.'

We left. My sister and I were taken to a hotel at the airport and I was carried up and put on the bed fully dressed, as I had asked. The pain was unbearable; I thought I was going mad. I could not move, and it was impossible to undress or get dressed again. I was counting the seconds until our flight left, and I could neither eat nor sleep. I prayed for help to endure it.

My sister was nervous. 'We will never get on that plane,' she said. 'They won't take someone so sick. You will have to go to hospital.'

'No, I must not. They cannot help me at the hospital; it is also made of stone, and they do not understand this,' I answered.

'I have to go home,' I went on. 'That is what I must do – go home to all the angels in my own house, to my own place. I shall manage. I shall pretend to be paralysed.'

And that is what I did. I got a wheelchair and was carried, moved, even put in the first class section. I have never had better service.

There was some confusion when we got to Fornebu Airport at Oslo, as no one could find this sick person's own wheelchair, but they lent me one and the problem was solved. This was a bright spot for my sister, who had been through hours of anxiety. Now she could laugh heartily with a sense of great relief over the mysteriously missing wheelchair.

After we had passed through customs, we were picked up by my husband, who brought us home, and according to my wishes I was put on the floor in the living room. Then something very strange happened. I physically felt the pain, anguish and sickness pour out of every pore in my body, together with a strong, unpleasant smell. I got better by the hour, and six hours later I could walk about in the house. After twelve hours I was well again.

Yes, I have learnt to protect myself now, even if I still forget sometimes. You must learn to do it too. Draw imaginary rings around yourself, several times a day if you can remember, golden or blue rings, and always seven times. Be aware of the fact that you often take on things which come from outside yourself, and therefore it is a golden rule to protect yourself often. Many people do not take responsibility for their own difficulties, and are not aware of the fact that negativity and irritation always come from within. They will try to push the blame on to someone else, either by verbally abusing them or by thinking, if it hadn't been for him or her, everything would have been fine. This is enough to make any sensitive person tired and nervous, and if we live under such stress for several years it can make us sick.

I will mention a couple of examples to show how little is needed.

I once asked a friend if I could borrow his typewriter because it was so much better than mine, and I sat relaxed and happy in his office, a couple of metres away from him, lost in my work. But after about three-quarters of an hour I suddenly felt uneasy and started to make mistakes. I paid attention to what was happening, and felt the irritation was building up in him; so I got up, thanked him for the use of his machine and said that I had finished.

'Oh good, that is great,' he said. 'I was just sitting here getting irritated because I remembered I have something I have to finish for tomorrow.'

Another time I had a client who slept over in one of my guest houses because we finished very late the day before. I had confronted him with something that we agreed he ought to get hold of and start working on. Well, I thought we had agreed, but something was left lying burning inside him. In the middle of the night I woke up with my heart pounding and feeling very restless. It was impossible to get back to sleep, so I got up, knelt by my altar and asked for protection. I prayed for my angel to be near me and take care of me, so that I could sleep and get strength for a new working day. Then I sent light and love to whoever was thinking of me. I felt calm again, and had a good night's sleep.

The next morning my client came in and told me that he had been lying awake thinking about all the things he hadn't cleared away and the things that he had made a mess of. 'And then, suddenly, I got so mad at you,' he said, and looked at me apologetically.

'But after half an hour those feelings disappeared and I went back to sleep. Now I feel ready to start clearing things up.'

I asked him what time this happened, and it was the time of my unrest and my prayer.

Have you, my reader, been breathing deeply and fully all the time you have been reading this? That is something you should exercise, it gives you so much more energy. Breathe deeply and be present in yourself.

Part of the reason for this book is to get as many readers as possible to breathe more deeply in order to get better contact with their real selves.

When we take care of people, animals and flowers with loving hands, that is also healing, in the same way that being touched by a closed, negative person is experienced as downright unpleasant. Many sick people have experienced that.

Some people give healing to the plants and flowers in their gardens without even thinking about it. We nourish and enjoy the flowers, their fragrance, their colour and fertility, and we automatically send joy and love, and the flowers feel it and take it in. They are as sensitive as we are. A lot of exciting literature has been written about this.

I was once given a good example of the way plants take in life force. I was helping to collect money for a good cause, and went from door to door with my collecting box. At one house I rang the bell too soon. As I put my finger on the bell, I felt that someone who lived there needed the money themselves, and the answer turned out to be, 'No, my dear. I haven't got a cent to give you.' The woman was about to close the door, but then opened it wide and said, 'No, do come in. I do want to give something. Come here and see my beautiful plant. You shall have a cutting, take two.'

The room was poorly furnished and was crying out for repairs, but in the corner, by the window, was a beautiful plant. It lit up the room. I thanked her, very touched, for the gift of two cuttings, and I put them carefully in my pocket. I sat there for a while talking to her before I carried on, wandering up and down stairs. I got home late and very tired, and fell straight into bed; but a couple of hours later I woke up with a start.

'Oh no – my plants! The cuttings in my pocket!' They were a sad sight, squashed and a bit brown at the edges, but I put them in water, held my hands over them and sent them light and life. The miracle happened again. The leaves straightened out, got their colour back and burst with life. They grew into a plant that I had for several years, until one autumn it was forgotten and left out in the garden and it froze. But it had shown me something important.

Rebirth

My growing interest in reincarnation made me take many different courses in self-development and rebirthing, which means to go back to one's own birth and sometimes even further, and I decided to learn more on this subject.

I wanted to study it very seriously. Rebirth is a fantastic tool which allows you to go very deep down into the unconscious of a person, to reach down under the level of verbal communication. It is a therapy which can give us a feeling of being born anew.

I had been reading psychology privately for many years, and as well as taking different courses in self-development, I had been in contact with lots of people as a voluntary social worker.

My experiences at rebirthing courses gave me a push into doing more. I found it to be the finest and purest therapy I had ever experienced. It opened a door to the secret depths that existed within me. This was really something of great value, something I wanted to share with other people. I thought of all those I had met during the years, who were troubled by deep anxiety and lack of self-confidence. I also thought of people I knew who suffered from repressed aggression. They all passed through my inner vision and I knew most of them would benefit from such an experience.

This form of therapy is very safe as long as it is performed by a therapist who has seriously worked through his or her own problems, and is secure in himself or herself, and is able to love him/herself and therefore to love other people.

We need experience and personal competence so we can help others meet their own anxieties or aggression. It is important to be able to handle whatever comes up, and there is no guarantee that the problems will be solved and disappear by themselves after one breathing lesson. We may need help to move on.

During my first course in rebirthing I made contact with

myself as a helpless two-year-old prisoner at the children's home. It was a terrible re-experience. I wept and cried out my despair, and experienced an intense rage towards all the foolish grown-ups around me.

There was a part of me that knew I was now a grown-up myself with a husband and a child, and that I was just taking part in a course; but the other part of me, the most real one, was a little two-year-old girl, completely helpless and unable to prevent what was happening around her. I was small and the others were big. You had to be big to be able to decide things in this world, to be seen and to be heard.

After the breathing – the rebirthing – I lay for a long time without moving, as if I were inside a cocoon. I felt that a light, constantly changing colour, protected me and I also felt an inexplicable love, as if I was surrounded by loving creatures.

What, then, is rebirthing? What do we do? What does it mean? To answer the last question first, rebirthing has its name because many people automatically go back into their earlier lives during the process. Some even go back to the moment when they were born, and experience their own birth into this life. For many people this may sound strange, but the proof that these experiences are not fantasy is that we have been able to ask the patient's mother afterwards if this was really the way it happened. Mothers are often alarmed to hear that their children have been able to report things they themselves have never told anybody in the family.

I could write many stories about this, and here are some:

A man of mature years came to me with a seemingly simple problem. He could remember nothing that had happened in his childhood before his first day at school.

'It is as if a window was opened there and then,' he told me. 'It was as if I only started to live and feel when I started school.'

The man had been to a small school, in a safe and close environment far from the city, with the same teacher for many years. She had been a warm and joyful woman with an open mind and great love for all her children. What surprised him was that even though his parents were good and fine people, he had never felt close to them. Why had he never felt loved and accepted? Why did he feel as if there were an abyss between them and him? Now he was an adult, they were good friends but nothing more.

We had a session with rebirthing. It was a strong experience. It was difficult to get him going, he seemed unable to breathe deeply. His thorax seemed completely blocked, and for a long time he was breathing only superficially. He disappeared and lay there without moving as if he was in a trance at times, and then his breathing became a bit better when I massaged his thorax. After an hour he at last got into a deeper breathing, while I gave him a light massage over the lungs.

Suddenly, it was as if he had passed through a wall. The breathing got deeper, but he did not seem to experience any other change. He was far away, as if asleep, but I suddenly felt the pressure on me easing up and it was easier to breathe.

The atmosphere in the room had been very heavy, and for the last half an hour I had been gasping for air like a fish out of water.

He breathed deeply and regularly for about a quarter of an hour, when he suddenly stopped completely.

He lay there as if he were dead. He became cold and pale, as if he had died a little, and he lay like that for a long time.

Then suddenly, with a jerk, he was back, curled up like a child, and he wept.

When his violent crying stopped at last, he turned over on his back, without opening his eyes, and began to breathe normally, radiating peace. After a while there was a sublime expression on his face, and I knew he was floating, in what I call contact with the universe and his true self. I let him lie like that for half an hour, then I called him back calmly. The story he told was dramatic.

He had experienced his own birth, and had been put aside, without anyone taking care of him. He was totally abandoned. It was a complete and absolute rejection: 'We don't want you.'

After this, for a long time he experienced only darkness, till suddenly he was met with a brilliant light surrounded by the most wonderful colours. He felt himself being lifted and carried as by invisible hands and surrounded by love, as in a heavenly existence.

He was touched and very happy when he left me and his whole body had loosened up and was at ease.

He was going to see his mother and ask her about what had happened at his birth.

A couple of days later he called me. His mother told him that they had believed him to be stillborn. He had shown no sign of life, and the midwife had wrapped him in a towel and put him on the windowsill. She had been completely occupied with the mother, who was in shock, and nobody had thought of taking the baby away. He had lain there for hours in the sun until at last someone had seen a movement in the little bundle. Alarmed, they unwrapped him and started to take care of him.

Now, he and his mother met in this common experience. She was shocked to hear that he had seen what happened. It had been a painful experience and she had never wanted to talk about it with him, nor to other people. Nor had she thought much about the fact that he kept to himself. 'I thought that it was your nature to be with the animals in the garden,' she said.

Anne-Lise came to me with a smile and told me that she had no problems, but that she thought this rebirthing sounded very exciting. 'I would very much like to see what it is like.' Her cousin had come to me earlier, and had clearly given her a colourful description.

Anne-Lise also had difficulty with her breathing. After two or three deep breaths, I had to remind her to breathe deeper by gently pulling her shoulders, or else I breathed deeply and clearly just beside her ear.

After forty minutes of deep breathing, she stopped completely with no muscle movement, not breathing at all. Then she suddenly cried out in anguish and panic, and at the same time she clung to me. She cried out, again and again, and then she cried, 'Help, get me out of here! Help me, help me!'

I put my arms around her and held her like the little child she was, without saying anything.

I just sat there, holding her till she calmed down, and for a moment she lay floating while I massaged her hands and feet.

After twenty minutes she was able to tell me that she had been born by Caesarean section. She had always known, but had never thought much about it. Now she had experienced herself being pulled out of the womb, and it came as a shock. It was felt like a wave of loneliness, coldness and anguish, because she had not been allowed to prepare in the natural way to leave her mother.

During a normal birth, the child knows what is going to happen. It senses, *Now it is getting too tight in here, I have to go into another existence.*

It turns around, communicating all the time with the mother, registering her feelings and thoughts, as it starts passing through the tunnel out into this world. The process takes as long as each child and each mother needs.

Birth is an adjustment process, a change to another form of existence for both mother and child. They will remain in symbiosis for some time until the child gets used to an existence as an independent individual.

The experience of being suddenly ripped out from the warm and safe place it is familiar with is very shocking for the child, and the shock is usually hidden deep down in the unconscious in order for the child to survive. It is too hurtful an experience to live with, but much of the damage can be repaired when we become conscious of it.

Fortunately, many midwives and also some doctors have learnt to put the child naked on the breast of the mother or father as soon as it is taken from the womb. This must be done as quickly as possible without wasting time washing the baby first. Weighing, measuring, washing, putting drops in the eyes should all be postponed, and no harm will be done, even if there is a delay in cutting the umbilical chord; but the baby is hurt by every second it is left alone in emptiness and absolute rejection. Furthermore, it is important for the baby to spend as much time as possible in close contact – skin to skin – with the mother or father. Baby massage is also a big help after such a shocking start in life.

Anne-Lise experienced the transition from her safe and warm existence in the womb to a cold, bright and busy new environment of loud voices and a total lack of security. In a matter of seconds and without warning, she was thrown into another reality. Her mother had not been prepared for a Caesarean, and the birth was a shocking experience for both mother and child.

This happened before we knew the importance of bodily contact. The baby was not taken to her mother until the next day, and I saw her cries and prayers for help 'to get out of there' as a need to be rescued from the big unsafe emptiness she found herself in when her mother was no longer there. It was a panicky prayer to get back into the womb or even to a life before her life on earth.

We know more now about the traumas which can occur after Caesarean sections, and we try to make such births as undramatic as possible. The baby is put onto the mother's bare breast, or perhaps the father's, or that of another person. It should preferably be one of the parents because the child will make a strong connection with the first person it has bodily contact with.

Anne-Lise came back a couple of times more, and managed to clear up a general feeling of insecurity that had always troubled her, but which she had tacitly accepted up until then.

Another young woman told me that her childhood remained a bleak memory, like a cool room bathed in pastel green light. She could not remember her father. She was born in Paris and had lived there during the first years of her life, but then her parents divorced. The mother moved back to Denmark with the daughter, who never saw her father again. Her mother did not talk much. She was bitter and reserved, and as often happens, the daughter became quiet and lived in her own dream world. One day her prince would come, should come, *had to* come. He would get her out of her loneliness, and the feeling of emptiness. But our princes and princesses come from within; they are a part of ourselves, they are our masculine or feminine sides coming out of the shadows, coming from the darkness and helping us to be free.

That young woman dreamed about her physical prince on a white horse.

We had a couple of breathing sessions together. Nothing much happened. After ten or twelve minutes she stopped breathing deeply and changed to a feeble, shallow breath and lay there almost as if she was unconscious.

The third time she came, she started the session the same way. On an impulse, I started to sing a French children's song to her, and she reacted immediately. Her breathing became deeper and after a while her eyelids started to vibrate. The expression on her face was that of a little child and she listened entranced, even after I stopped singing. She was there as a small child in Paris with her beloved dad. After the session, happy and excited, she told me what she had experienced. She had seen herself with her father. She could still hear his laughter in her ears. He had often sung to her, something her mother had never done. The joy had disappeared with him.

We talked about how it had been necessary for her to put a lid on the memory of her father. Losing him had been too hard for her to bear.

It was too late to go and see him, as he was no longer here on earth, but through the breathing sessions and with her inner helper she got out of that closed room.

She became one of my first students, a strong and eager rebirther.

It is a fact that we are most easily impressed by what happens to us at the very beginning of our life here on earth. From the beginning of the period in the womb, and over the first two or three years of life, we are as impressionable as wax and easy to shape – I am tempted to say, much too easy. We are formed by the world we live in, a world often filled with frustrated, restless people. We take the imprint of our parents and siblings, of our surroundings and their meanings, of ways of being, body language – everything makes deep impressions.

Once I had a woman living with me in intensive therapy for a whole week. She had great difficulty in handling everyday life with her husband and children. Her nerves were in very bad shape and she started to behave strangely, talking incoherently and telling fantastic stories to her husband's business colleagues. It became difficult and very embarrassing for everybody and there was talk of having her institutionalised for a while. A friend of the family told them about me and persuaded them to contact me first. She came from abroad so it had to be intensive treatment, and I knew it would be a challenging and interesting week.

She was a tiny, beautiful little person, charming and brightly intelligent, but she projected an exceptional insecurity. She had a habit of throwing quick glances around, as if to check the reactions of others to her behaviour, and she did everything in order to avoid displeasing anybody. Her husband was an enterprising businessman in an important position. He made great demands on himself and everybody else, and had little understanding for what he called weakness. His impatience had obviously aggravated her condition.

Through rebirthing breathing sessions we worked our way back to her own youth, and she started to cry. She actually cried for three days while she relived what she felt to be most painful. Her father had been her god; she admired him and loved him and wanted so much to talk to him, show him things and discuss things with him.

He just laughed at her, not disdainfully or with any hint of rejection, but he laughed, shaking his head, told her that she was sweet and she was his little doll, and went on with his reading or his work. He was occupied with his own adult world and never had anything to say to her. He never listened to her. She remained a little doll, a toy or an ornament for her parents. This is a fate common to many small girls, especially from southern countries.

She grew up to become graceful and coquettish, as her parents expected her to be. She suppressed her independent thoughts and married a dominating man who was an exact copy of her father, and she carried on suppressing her abilities. She played the role of the little doll, the doll her husband had married and wanted her to be. It worked for a while, for some years even, but then things started to crack, as they often do when we try to suppress our real character.

We would have liked to have more than a week together, she and I, but the days that we did have brought her closer to her real self. The woman I drove to the airport was a grown-up woman with much more self-confidence, and she was smiling when she left. She was looking forward to getting to know her family from another angle. She was also very determined to go on drawing and painting. We had been painting quite a lot during the week and she was good at it.

The moral, if you can handle the word moral without seeing it negatively, is never laugh at a child. Laugh *with* them when they play and when they tell you something they think funny, but never laugh *at* them. Take them seriously: listen with interest to what they want to share with you from the very beginning.

You can learn more important things from them than you can from newspapers and television. Don't talk to them, talk with them.

If you listen to them and are present in yourself when you are with them, you will give them self-confidence and they will feel precious. There is no reason to look down on children. They are not yet harmed by the influences of society, and they probably have more wisdom to pass on to you than you can give to them because they have not yet forgotten what they brought with them from the other side.

You should honour their higher self and talk politely to them. Show that you respect them, the way you want to be respected.

If you laugh at them, they feel silly and think that they are being made fun of. They learn that to laugh at someone is acceptable; then the way is clear for them to play games to gain attention, to behave artificially, to make sarcastic remarks about themselves and others. Sarcasm is such a widely admired technique in our insensitive society. And when we have been down this road we become well locked up within ourselves, and the table is set for conflict.

The Secret of Breath

I want to talk some more about rebirthing, the session of breathing when you learn to free the breath. It is a safe, soft, and powerful way to breathe.

What we do is to breathe deeply and continuously, without any stop between breathing in and breathing out, for a period of between forty and sixty minutes. It is important to fill the lungs completely and then let the air out without forcing it. Breathe in and let go, and at every exhalation relax the muscles and let go of your thoughts. The thoughts will come back, and you let go of them again and again.

Every time you feel tension in a muscle, visualise yourself entering into that muscle, and release the tension as best you can at every exhalation.

If you have never participated in any form of breathing session before, you should be careful about trying it on your own.

You may well breathe continuously and fully for about twenty times, breathing in and exhaling, but after that you should stop for a while. If you feel yourself getting dizzy or if you feel a tingling in your forehead, these are signs that you exist on superficial breathing. It means that your breathing is deficient. You get too little oxygen, too little energy. Be good to yourself and get used to breathing more deeply, and do twenty continuous deep breathings every now and then; but don't start rebirthing on your own.

It is important to have an experienced rebirther with you for the first twenty times. We enter such deep processes when we manage to let go that it is not good to be alone. But breathing continuously twenty times, several times a day, will improve the quality of your life.

At first, rebirthing leads to less stress and a greater joy of life. It helps you to meet fear and aggression and helps free you from them, and you will get stronger. Rebirthing does not change your life, it is you who do that. It is your thoughts that form and shape your life, but rebirthing helps to loosen up negative, heavy mental substance and stiffness in the muscles, and this, in time, will improve your life.

What is really happening physiologically when we breathe continuously in this way?

We supply more oxygen (O_2) to the blood. We exhale carbon dioxide (CO_2). This can create a tingling feeling in fingers, lips and skin. It is quite safe, but in the old days when someone hyperventilated, or exhaled more carbon dioxide than usual, it was treated as hysteria.

As we lie on our backs during breathing sessions, it does not matter if we get a bit dizzy in the beginning, and we hardly notice it, but we can sometimes feel our bodies getting heavy and restless. Our emotions and defences start reacting. Many still believe that hyperventilating is dangerous, but recent research proves the opposite.

The word hyperventilating comes from the words *hyper* – exaggerated, more than normal, and *ventilate* – to breathe.

When we breathe continuously using all our lung capacity over a period of time without moving our bodies, thus using little oxygen, the carbon dioxide content in the blood is reduced. The concentration of oxygen increases, but only slightly, and this causes the blood vessels in the brain and in the skin to contract. The method is used in hospitals during brain operations and for serious head injuries, and haemorrhages in the head, but it is carried out artificially by means of a respirator.

It is the amount of CO_2 in the blood that makes us take the trouble to breathe. When living organisms, whether animals or people, use oxygen, our body metabolisms produce carbon dioxide as a waste product.

Green plants, on the other hand, transform CO_2 into oxygen during the day by a process called photosynthesis. They clear the air for us. During the night they consume a small amount of oxygen, but much less than they produce during a day.

No one needs to be afraid of getting too little blood to the brain, which will always get what it needs, about 750 ml per minute, through a mechanism called auto-regulation.

This mechanism always functions well in healthy people, and it is only with extremely low blood pressure and in terminally ill patients that auto-regulation may fail. I believe it is more dangerous, or rather more harmful, to breathe too little than it is to hyperventilate.

Hypo means 'under', or too little, and most people hypoventilate. Many physical illnesses are caused by too small a supply of oxygen to the cells.

My experience with my patients is that as soon as I make them breathe more deeply they experience a better quality of life and their health improves.

Pains and tensions in the body will also diminish, as long as we manage to keep up the habit of deeper breathing.

When I started this therapy, which is a combination of psychotherapy, healing and deep breathing, no one in Norway was providing instruction in it. Nor were there any practising rebirthers in the country, so it was necessary to go abroad, and I did it with pleasure. I have always found it exciting and enriching to meet other cultures. I got my training in the USA, in India and in Sweden. It was exciting, and I was even more enthusiastic when I started to practise this form of therapy myself.

The results were quick to come. I was deeply touched and grateful for all the things that happened in the wake of the breathing sessions.

I continued to work as a silversmith and enamel painter half the time because I was very fond of my work. It was good to create things with my hands, and I did not actively seek other clients. Those who are going to come to me will come anyway, I thought, and they did. The grapevine was so effective that I had to say to those who did come, 'Don't talk about me, I have no time for more clients.' But the day came when I had to quit my job as a silversmith. I chose to devote all my time to the therapy, and it gave me so much back that each day was a joy. For several years I commuted between Oslo and Copenhagen. In the sixties, there was more interest in alternative treatment in Denmark than in Norway and it was in Copenhagen that I was asked to give seminars. It was there that I got my first students in rebirthing, which was very inspiring. The seminar was a success. I decided it must be possible to do this in Norway too, and after some years, after having been asked repeatedly, I started to teach there too.

In Copenhagen I started regression therapy because I was constantly being asked to. I had been hesitant about regressions. If you are supposed to remember anything from a past life, it will come up in an ordinary rebirthing, I thought. I also had the feeling that such requests were made more out of curiosity than from a deep and honest wish for personal growth. Usually I said no, and I listened to the tone of people's voices when they called me and asked for regression. If I sensed that it was just out of curiosity, I stuck to my decision and told them that I only worked with people who had a serious desire to work through their difficulties and challenges in this life.

One of those I did accept was Poul. He was in his fifties and was the father of another client of mine, Birgith, whom I had been working with for about a year. She was severely hampered by a childhood marked by her father's continual fits of rage. Poul had a business which he managed alone with only a little extra help from time to time.

He was afflicted with headaches, which came and went and made it difficult for him to manage his work. When he came to me, I started him up with deep breathing, but this did not work very well. After only three or four deep breaths, he 'disappeared', and was barely breathing at all. I then led him over the 'rainbow bridge', as I call it when I put people into a trance.

'You are now in a former life,' I told him, and waited eagerly to find out where he was going to take us. It became a violent session. He was back in a port area in London, where he worked as a docker. He spoke in broad English and his voice was coarser and deeper than the one he had in this life. That he spoke English was strange in itself, as in his present life he could not speak this language.

In London he was married to a woman he saw little of. He led a sad life and was continually in trouble. He got into fights after too many pints at the pub. I asked him to go back to his childhood in that life and he saw himself with a father who often mistreated him in fits of rage. Once he came close to being killed. He was hit on the head with a bottle and lay in a coma for quite some time. Later, as a seventeen-year-old, he left his home after a violent confrontation with his father. I sat by Poul while he told about this and watched his expressions. They varied between rage and despair. When he came to the confrontation with his father, he was screaming with all his might, and he lifted his hands and put them around my neck in an iron grip. I had no opportunity to loosen the grip, nor could I speak.

He'll let go, I thought. It is not meant to end this way. But he held on, and I was about to lose consciousness.

'Lord,' I prayed, 'if this is what is meant to be, I accept that I must die now.'

In the same moment as the prayer was thought, Poul let go. His hands fell onto his breast, his face became peaceful and he breathed calmly. He was floating.

When at last I brought him back, he remembered only the sadness of the docks and that his father had been brutal to his mother. He had moved between them, felt a blow to his head and saw a light lifting him out of the dark.

'I saw the same light just now,' he said. 'It was as if I was floating in a divine light. I don't believe in God, but that was strange! I don't know what to say or think.'

'You don't have to say anything,' I said. 'Things will fall into place after a while. There are lots of things within us that we don't have any contact with. They are hidden inside us and in the days to come, many pictures may emerge from memory.'

I asked him how he was feeling; he shook his head and smiled warmly at me. 'I am terribly tired, but I feel better than I can ever remember. I feel warm and pleasant in the whole of my body, and it is tingling right down to my toes. Strange!' He shook his head again and told me that he had always been worried about his anger, and feared he might hurt somebody seriously. But now he was filled with peace and an unknown joy. He had a feeling of not being alone.

'We each have an angel,' I told him. 'Address your angel, it is very eager to get in contact with you.' Maybe he did.

He and his daughter were now both in therapy with me. She told me that he no longer had fits of rage. He said that his headaches were gone and he felt much fitter and more harmonious. He came back another three times, and by then he was just doing the breathing session, freeing the breath. He was breathing deeply and for long periods without stopping, and he felt very well after each session. I followed his progress through his daughter who came to me for another year, and at the end of that time he was still feeling fit and at peace with himself.

I could have told him about his assault on me, but I chose not to. It was important not to disturb his harmony and it could have created a fear. Now everything was as it should be, and I am sure that both his angel and mine were with us that day. After experiencing a light such as Poul did, we change completely. He spoke about the light with wonder and joy, and he had a new light in his eyes.

Birgith came regularly for breathing and conversation. She became more self-reliant and decided to continue her studies and enter a school for alternative therapy, and I encouraged her to do so, wished her well and went back to Norway. Two weeks later she called me, very happy, and told me that she had been accepted at the school.

It was now the summer holidays and I did not go back to Denmark for ten weeks; but one day in August, when I was out walking my dog, Birgith suddenly appeared to me. I saw her face clearly, and then I saw her walking along the sidewalk with a letter in her hand that she was going to post.

I stopped, lifted both hands in the direction where I felt she was, and thought, Stop, Birgith, don't do it! You are heading down the wrong track.

I stood there for a while until her image disappeared, then I put away my thoughts of her and enjoyed my walk in the woods.

Back home, I picked up the phone and called her. She was in high spirits and happy to have someone to talk to. She told me that she had felt depressed for a couple of weeks and had started to doubt that she would be able to go through with her studies. She had written a letter to the school telling them she would not be able to attend, but on her way to the letter box a light that she could not pass through had stopped her. She turned around and went home.

Who doubts that we have power? We have enormous powers! But we have to believe in them, believe in ourselves and remember that we are divine beings.

We are a part of God, with talents and power for everything. It is up to us to take care of our talents and develop them in faith, devotion and love, in work for humanity and our own growth. We create ourselves anew with every moment, and we create our world. The world is not as it is, it is as I am; you create yours and I create mine. Everything depends on our own way of thinking, our attitude. We all have full responsibility for our own lives and our influence on ourselves and the world around us.

It is up to us how we interpret everything that is being said, and how we relate to what is happening. Every single thought creates positivism or negativity. We are continually creating.

We can choose to participate actively in our own life, or we can run away from it. We have the potential to close off, suppress what is going on inside us and live the lives of others more than our own by being preoccupied with what everybody else says and does. We can pass most of our free time in front of the TV, occupy ourselves with gossip from papers and magazines, fill the time with empty chat or frenetic activity, and grab the phone desperately every time it gets quiet inside us.

Alternatively we can choose to contact the silence, to be present in ourselves, to breathe in deeply and feel what is in the depths within, find our primitive force and inner wisdom, listen to the voice of the soul.

Choose to live your life and *be*. Choose to say, 'I am.' Ask, 'What do I want? What do I want with my life?'

This demands a greater effort. It demands courage and strength, but there is so much wisdom deep inside you, it is important to listen to it and live the life you decided to live before you incarnated on earth. If deep feelings of anxiety, anger and loss should surface, you will have the ability and the power to meet them and breathe through them. Further inside yourself you will find the joy of life, the joy of being alive. You will be able to create your life and become the one you were supposed to be. 'As your days are, so shall your strength be.'

Everybody has his own Angel

One of my clients, a young woman, came to see me quite often. She and her husband had troubles, and she said that she felt it was like being in a refuge to be with me, just to be there. She attended some of my classes, and this apparently became too much for her husband. He felt rejected and misunderstood, and one day he came to see me to tell me that it had to stop. He did not want her to come to me anymore. He did not want me to contact her, and he had forbidden her to call me or come to see me.

I solved this in my own way. I started to pray for them several times a day and sent them love and light.

One day, four months later, my angel appeared and said, 'Go to the letter box.'

'No, it is too early, it is only ten o'clock.'

'Go to the letter box!'

Fine… I knew I had to obey.

I put on a jacket and went down to the porch, and there coming towards me was my client, whom I hadn't seen for quite some time, but who had been with me every day. She was on the point of passing, looking down, not daring to speak, when it was as if we were struck by the light, with the power of lightning. It went through me from the top of my head to my feet, and I had difficulty keeping my balance. At that moment I was filled with an enormous energy and joy, but I pretended that nothing had happened and just smiled at her. I knew she was afraid of such events, but as it turned out she had the same experience. She looked at me with wide eyes and exclaimed, 'What was that? I felt so strange.'

I just laughed and said, 'Maybe it was your angel who brought you here. I have been thinking so much about you, it is so good to see you.'

Her eyes met mine and her face relaxed. She was suddenly very close. 'You have sent us much light,' she said. 'I have felt it. Things are going much better between us.'

It was another confirmation of the strength of prayers, and the fact that light and love also reach those who are shut off from it.

The light that hit us was a manifestation of the universal power which is there for everybody to tap into. We experienced one of the small miracles, which often happen. The light is with us, but usually we don't notice it because we are not at one with ourselves. We are so preoccupied with everything happening around us that we forget our own inner worlds.

When we remember that we are divine, we own a power which can send energies to the other side of the earth if need be. We must learn to be confident without needing to understand it. This is something we can learn from our children before they become influenced by all the grown-ups around them.

One of my clients received a cry for help from her husband. He was on a business trip to the Far East, as he had an important mission there, but he completely collapsed and was unable to negotiate. He had great difficulty breathing, could hardly speak a word and could neither eat nor drink. He had been to see a doctor, but it was a doctor of a different calibre from ours. He had looked at him calmly and said in the most matter-of-fact way, 'I can do nothing to help here; other forces are needed.'

So the call came through to me. Fortunately I knew the man; he had come to me for healing earlier. I had him in my heart, and we agreed on a time for him to lie on his bed at the hotel to received healing. I contacted my sister and another woman, who are both strong senders, and we sat, each of us in our own home, and sent love, light and healing to him for fifteen minutes.

A couple of hours later I had a phone call from a happy voice, and in high spirits he told me that the healing had been fantastic. His room had become lighter, he had felt uplifted and held, and both the pain and the anguish had disappeared. When the fifteen minutes had passed he got up from his bed feeling refreshed and well. His throat felt open and relaxed and he was filled with energy and zest for life. After having taken a shower he went downstairs to the dining room, whistling, and had a substantial lunch with his business associates. They were very surprised and asked, 'What on earth happened to you?'

He had just laughed and said, 'There is so much here on earth that we don't understand.'

Healing can be done from a distance; distance does not restrict our power. Reflect a little while upon the potential that we possess. The power to heal is not limited to just a few people. It seems that everybody has the possibility to develop these gifts. The strength of individuals may vary, but it is clear that we only use a small part of our potential.

Allow yourself to use your whole potential. For your own good, build up a respect for yourself as the unique being you arc. The talents we don't use will wither and fade. Man is created for challenges.

Here is another example of power. I had a woman in for a rebirthing session, and after having had contact with a former life, she lay there floating for a while. There were angels around us and the room was filled with a dim light. It was more than my stereo player could take – a cloud of smoke came out of the amplifier and it packed up. Later we discovered that the same thing had happened to her hearing aid.

When we get in touch with the divine energies within us, the power discharges are enormous. This was not the only time my amplifier was destroyed. Unfortunately, it has become an expense I have to deal with.

On another occasion, the set turned itself on when my hand was still almost a metre away from it.

Oh yes. We have power, and that is why it is so important to use it correctly.

For a long time. I drove around in a wreck of a car, sustained mainly by power and prayer.

When I was stopped at a control point one day, it just gave up. The man who had stopped me checked out various functions, but nothing worked. He tried to start the car, but it was impossible. They checked everything and all they got was a faint reaction from one of the cylinders.

That could be a little goodbye to me from the car, I thought. ('Goodbye, Sissel. We have had much fun together. There is an end to everything.)

'I've never seen anything like it!' he shouted at me furiously. He got more and more angry; it became quite amusing.

'Can't I just drive home?' I asked him.

'Not another metre,' he snarled, and he cut off the number plates dramatically.

I have many stories about cars, just as fantastic, but this little book is not supposed to be about cars.

We must always work in the service of good. If we don't, we only hurt ourselves. Everything we do comes back to us, whether we believe it or not; such is the law of karma, the law of retaliation.

If we have gratitude, joy and prayers for protection, we can be there for each other and create a good world to live in. We can help others, not by worrying, but by believing that everything will turn out well. If we imagine all the horrible things which might happen, we actually help to manifest them. Then they might very well happen and we will have created the problems ourselves.

Worry also creates negativity. If we worry about somebody we pull negativity onto that person.

If you pray with sorrow and worry for a friend lying sick in his bed, his guardian angel will believe that that is how it should be, and will therefore help to keep him there. On the other hand, if you pray for him with joy and at the same time imagine him healthy, happy and strong, his angel will help him recover.

Again, remember this. We create our world. The world is not as it is. It is as I am.

A human life can be compared to a river on its way to the sea, just as we are on our way back to God.

Imagine yourself as a piece of bark floating on this river. At times you will be pulled down into a whirlpool, but you will come up again into the sunlight and dance on top of the glittering surface of the water. At other times, you might end up in a backwater and turn around there for a long time, until a violent shower forces you back into the stream to continue your path through life.

Change takes time and our evolution is slow, but if we manage to stay centred in ourselves, changes will occur all the time. It is like the drop of water hollowing out the stone; by working with ourselves, we can increase our psychic capacities more than a thousandfold. We evolve into consciously working healers on earth, and the more there are of us, the greater our power.

This can easily be seen when we meditate together in a group. The universal power can be so strongly with us that it feels as if the ceiling is lifting, and the healing we send out at that point is very strong. Listen to your soul, not to your ego.

The ego, or personality, may wish for riches and power. The ego is usually acting out of fear, from the solar plexus. It is afraid that it won't get enough of the worldly goods. It is afraid of hunger, suffering and distress, weakness, insignificance, exposure and death. Those fears make us gather money, which gives us an illusion of safety. If, instead, we let go of fear and open our hands, we see that the more we give, the more we get back.

The thing that hinders some people is the lack of faith. Each of us has the choice of putting up barriers, but your angel cannot reach you if you are not in contact with yourself. Many books have been written about people who talk with angels.

Everybody can do it; our bodies are our temples. When we make ourselves open for contact with our angels, we open ourselves up to lives where we are no longer alone. We each have our guardian angel, and your angel will guide and protect you.

Our angels wait patiently for us to pray for and seek contact with them. They let us do stupid and completely wrong things, if that is what we want, because that gives us experience and the potential to learn from our mistakes. They never interfere in our lives and our actions unless they are encouraged to do so. They never accuse us, nor do they have any opinion about what is right or wrong.

They wait for us to be receptive and then they are there immediately.

For small children it is different. From the moment we are born, the angels are near us. Sometimes they are there with mother and child through the whole of a pregnancy. This depends on what the individual child has decided before returning to earth to be incarnated here.

My angel often talks to me, and the times when I listen and do as I'm told, everything turns out well. When I follow my own course through absent-mindedness or stubbornness, things go very wrong.

What often happens is that we forget to pray for and give thanks for the help that we get.

How many times my angel has helped me is something I hardly know. There is one incident I would like to relate because it remains vividly in my mind.

I had been to see some friends in Eggedal in the Norwegian mountains, and in the evening I was going to drive on to Krøderen. I decided to drive over the mountain to save time.

It was a moonlit night, freezing cold, and I went off in an optimistic mood. Suddenly, I had to turn to avoid a hole in the road and the car slid sideways. One wheel ended up in the ditch and the car was left resting on its axle. No matter what I did, it was stuck.

I gathered myself together, prayed for help and sent thanks for the help which would come. I waited for five minutes, then a snow-scooter appeared with four men on board – four men on a tiny scooter.

They laughed and pulled my car up onto the road and then disappeared in a cloud of snow.

Angels? I called them that and thanked them warmly for their help.

They smiled and said, 'Yes, we are angels.'

They had certainly come as an answer to my prayer. Night had already fallen and they were the only living beings I saw on that whole trip. I continued on my way, singing and sending my thanks.

Up on the mountain I was overwhelmed by the beauty and had to get out of the car to take it all in – the twinkling stars, the moonlight throwing a magic light over mountain and valley, the shining snow and the friendly lights from the houses by the side of Lake Kroderen down at the bottom of the valley. I felt chosen and blessed to be able to experience this. I was taken care of.

Behind the next bend, a new challenge waited for me. The road in front of me was covered over by a snowdrift about a metre and a half high. I had no shovel in the car and it was impossible to turn around because the road was too narrow. I looked up to heaven for help, and up there I saw my star shining right above my head. Once again I sent my thanks and interpreted it as a sign. Reversing a little, I put the car in 'Drive' and gave it everything, shooting through the drift like a rocket.

It was impossible, but it proved to be possible. Maybe there are more angels out in God's natural world than in all the big cities.

It occurred to me that everything seems stronger when we are outdoors. Maybe there aren't any more angels out there, but people get more in touch with themselves and it is easier to feel the presence of God.

A friend told me this story. She and her parents met with an angel on Hardangervidda, another of Norway's large mountains.

They were on a trip and driving towards the little township of Odda, when they picked up a young man hiking. He looked quite normal, but he carried no backpack, nor anything else.

On the way down to Odda, he entertained them in a lively way. He said that mankind had to turn to God. For a long time they had turned away from God, but the time had come to turn back.

He vibrated light and warmth, and they appreciated his company very much so they asked him if he would go further with them.

'No, thank you, I am returning to the mountain,' he said, and at that moment he disappeared into thin air.

My friend's father was completely confused and wanted to stop at the first petrol station, because this was not a normal event for him.

He confided in the attendant at the petrol station. The man just stood there, looking at them.

'What do you think of that, then?' my friend asked him. She thought he didn't show much of a reaction.

'Well, what can I say?' he replied. 'I probably would have found you a bit strange, if it was not for the fact that six cars have stopped here already today with the same story.'

On one occasion when my guardian angel gave me a warning, I was on my way home after working in Copenhagen. I was sitting at Kastrup Airport, waiting to board the plane, when I suddenly felt that something was wrong. It was something to do with the plane's engine.

What should I do? Should I tell somebody? No, no one would believe me. Should I take another plane? But then, what about the other people? I told my angel, 'If I get on board this plane and pray, then no accident will happen.' I boarded the plane and we taxied out onto the runway, then sat there for quite some time. After half an hour we heard the pilot's voice over the intercom. 'We have found a fault in the engine, we have to change to another plane.'

Meditation

It was a sparkling bright winter morning, the beginning of the weekend. Outside, snow crystals were twinkling and Christmas lights hung like pearls on the trees in the garden. The daylight had not yet reached its full power. Ratcha, my dog, was barking. Someone was at the door. One of my students arrived with a shining, long-stemmed rose.

'It is important to listen to one's inspiration,' he said. 'I had a strong sense that I should come here today. We are so grateful for all we get here. It is something basic, something essential. Many important matters have been written about, but very often the essence is missing. That is what we get here from you. You teach us to be present within ourselves, all the time. We are striving with our own problems, but we have the foundation we need.'

This was the answer to my questions – my prayer to my angel. I had been asking it again that morning; for how long I know not:

'Why should I write this book? There are so many other things I would like to do – things I could do better! I have never liked talking; I am no good at it. Let others who want to speak do so, and let those who know how to write do that.' So when Morten came with the rose it was both a reminder and an encouragement.

I went in and found my writing gear; that weekend I resolved to work on my book. I would just let come what came forth, with confidence that it was right to share the things that lay within me.

Once, a long time ago, a master told me, 'You will go home and teach meditation and help those who come to you find the way into themselves, and find the way back to the divine.'

'I can't.' I said. 'Allow me to be spared from this. They can find the way well enough on their own.'

'No, you shall do this,' said the master, 'and you will start as soon as you get home.'

I went home, but I didn't tell anybody. Strangely enough, people started to come and ask me to teach meditation. I answered, hesitantly, 'I will think about it.'

One Monday, my angel's patience came to an end. During my morning meditation, I received a clear message. 'You must start today!'

With my five planets in Aries, I could not help arguing. 'Yes, but it is too short notice. We can't start today. Nobody would possibly come.'

'You will start today!'

Well, I had to try. I telephoned all those who had asked for meditation recently. They were all available. They were happy, they came and others with them, that same evening. It was good and it was right. I realised how much many of them benefited from it, and many things happened. The atmosphere was warm and intimate and there was growth for all of us.

After this, I had groups for meditation every Monday in Oslo and in Soon.

When, after some years, I started having these gatherings only in Soon, one of the regulars told me miserably, 'Now I am losing my church!'

When we are together in meditation, in a way we are building a church. We create a cathedral of light – a well of light – which grows and grows, bigger and bigger, until it stretches out far beyond the walls of the house. The light extends out further and further, like ripples on water, till it meets with light from other groups spread out over the whole world. We serve humanity, our living earth, and we also serve our own growth and ourselves. We can be servants of the world, help to pull in light and energy, love from God, from the universe, and send it to everything and everyone around us.

How do we meditate? We put our minds at rest. We open up to the light, the power and the love from the universe itself. We try consciously to reach our innermost centre, the seed of our being, in order to find our primitive force and forgotten wisdom – the wisdom we have possessed from the beginning of time. It is hidden deep within us and it is up to us to open up to it.

Within us, there is a clear, pure flame burning. This is the real, essential I, the spark that emanated from God in the beginning, a part of God himself. We must find our way back to it. Only when we are in contact with this flame can we each live our real life the way it was meant to be, the way we decided it would be before we chose our parents and let ourselves be born into this incarnation and our life on earth.

Had we been able to bring with us this clairvoyance and our memory of past lives, things would have been easier. Then we could have avoided closing ourselves off, blocking out our feelings and suppressing them by cementing them into stomach, neck or legs.

We might have tackled adversity much better, because we would have remembered the reason for our coming here this time and that this was our own choice.

But then, we would not have learnt our lessons. We have to struggle in order to gain the experience we need.

As it is now, we use much of our time and energy fighting against all the things that scare us, all the adversities. We close off and block out all the terrible things, all the fears, the inadequacies we believe to be true but which come from ourselves, from our fear of not being good enough, not being worthy enough for others to like us and love us.

It is when we are fighting against all this that things really get difficult. We are like drowning people who are desperately fighting, panting and puffing, swallowing water and sinking, instead of taking deep, calm breaths and allowing ourselves just to float and be carried by the water.

In our form of light meditation, we work very consciously. The key words are acceptance, tolerance and love. In this meditation we aim to get into contact with the tiny, unprotected child in ourselves, the child who is hiding beneath the fear, the shame, the doubt and the judgements. We hold the little child and give it love, at the same time filling ourselves with light from the universe, filling ourselves with the highest, purest light, the divine, with Christ – consciousness.

Give yourself the gift of love. Feel how it fills you, imagine holding the child within you, believe in it.

The more love and faith you give to yourself, the more you

will be able to open up, you will meet with your child and it will be easier to reach your higher self. No matter how much darkness you have within you, know that you are also light. We are both darkness and light. There is no day without a night, no front without a back. We are earth and sky. Accept your darkness and transform it, little by little, into energy. Have patience.

You are a part of God. Every time we breathe in, we fill ourselves with light, again and again; fill every cell of the body. Every time we breathe out, we let go of all the thoughts we no longer want.

Do not worry because it is difficult to let go of the thoughts, just let them go, again and again, every time you exhale, and imagine at the same time that you are letting go of negativity and sickness.

You must empty yourself completely of everything which disturbs your peace. Only you, your angel, the universe and God exist. Your body is your temple; you live within it twenty-four hours a day. Fill it with love.

After this kind of joint meditation, we send healing to all those who have asked for it and we send light and love to planet earth, to people and animals, then we are in silence ourselves before God. We are silent in ourselves and silent for ourselves.

We are, I am.

Then we become receivers, open to information from our own angel, the master, from God and from the universe.

This form of meditation that we use has evolved and crystallised from all the different forms of meditation that I have seen and tried in my permanent search for what is right for me.

I don't believe that only one form of meditation is right and others are wrong, but not all forms are suitable for everyone. We seek and find the one that is best for us. Then we can find strength.

If you have never practised meditation, it can be useful to exercise the breathing first.

Sit down on a chair, in a comfortable position, with your back straight, your legs parallel and your feet flat on the floor, preferably without shoes in order to get a better earth-contact. Otherwise you can sit on the floor in the lotus position, which means you sit with crossed legs and the feet as close to the body as possible.

You can use the diamond position, sitting on a cushion or a low stool with bent knees turned backwards. Suitable stools can be bought in many yoga centres, or you can make one yourself.

Push your lower back a bit forward to keep your back straight. Sit on the sitting nodes, not on your caudal vertebra. The sitting nodes are the round bones you can feel when you sit on your hands.

It is important to sit with a straight back and in a comfortable position where you won't tire easily. Bring your body to rest. It can be helpful to tighten the muscles in the body and then let them go. Do this several times, it gives you better contact with your body and makes it easier to feel when you have let go. If your body is very tense, you should do it several times a day; do it again and again, tighten and let go, tighten and let go. This is good for both body and mind.

It is an exercise used by many yogis in India, and who would not want the kind of contact with the body that they have. The exercise will not take away any of your 'precious' time, as you can do it anywhere and any time, at school or on the job, in your car or on the bus – even when you are bored stiff at a never-ending meeting. These are also good times for training yourself in deep, full breathing.

And now for the breathing.

Lift your left arm and place your fore and middle fingers on the third eye, the point between and a little above eyes. Close the right nostril with the ring finger. Breathe in through the left nostril, taking as much time as possible for the inhalation. Fill your lungs completely. Count to yourself, one, two, three, four, five, six, so you can keep up a constant rhythm. After you have inhaled, hold your breath for the same length of time that you used for breathing in: one, two, three, four, five, six. Now put your thumb on the left nostril and exhale through the right, taking the same length of time for exhalation as you did for the inhalation and for holding your breath. One, two, three, four, five, six. Wait for two seconds, then breathe in through the right nostril, filling the lungs completely.

Once again, use the same timing: one, two, three, four, five, six. Hold your breath as long again, then put your ring finger back on the right nostril, take away the thumb from the left and exhale in the same time span.

In the convents in Tibet they call these two inhalations and exhalations one breath, and they consider it very important to exercise this breathing technique before starting to meditate.

You continue this form of breathing for at least ten minutes, but you can keep going for half an hour or longer. Practice makes you the master and you will get a deep and satisfying contact with your inner self.

Remember that after you have exhaled there is a two-second pause. Breath in through your left nostril, hold your breath for the same length of time, use the timing again to breathe out through the right nostril. Wait for two seconds, breathe in, hold, breathe out, wait for two seconds again and continue. It will get easier and more exciting as you learn to master this form of breathing, and you will have a feeling of heaviness and calm throughout your body.

After a while you can feel a sort of tingling in your third eye, and you will feel that it is easier to let go of your thoughts. This form of breathing is also called *withheld breath*, and can be helpful in letting us contact our higher consciousness.

When you start to meditate, I want to remind you that the important thing is not the quantity but the quality. To begin with, it is sufficient to meditate for five or ten minutes. Don't overdo it, because then it will be easier to give up. It is a process of adaptation. Meditation does not suit everybody, but the breathing is always good for you. I repeat this ad nauseam: a deep, complete breathing improves the quality of life for everyone.

Just as important as these breathing exercises is the ability to ground yourself – to get the feeling of being present in your body. Most people do not have this grounding; our consciousness is somewhere high above our heads.

Here is an exercise that you can use.

Stand up with your feet parallel and your arms hanging down. When you breathe in, you lift your arms out to the sides with your palms turned upwards, and then up above your head. Bend your wrists and turn your palms down and bring the arms down in front of the body while you breathe out. Feel your body become heavy and peaceful.

This is not an exercise to be done quickly. Breathe calmly and deeply while you do it. Give yourself time and attention.

Imagine that you are pulling your energies downwards, down into your belly, and feel that you are standing firmly on the ground. You ground yourself, then anchor yourself while you breathe out and bring the hands down. You feel heavy in your hips and your legs. You stand firmly on the ground. You are a part of our wonderful, living planet, a link between earth and heaven, and you are the one to pull heaven down to earth.

You can also use another good grounding exercise.

You start out as before, standing with feet parallel and hands at the sides.

Imagine, visualise, that you have a ball of red rope in your belly, in the hara centre, below the navel. Breathe in, and in breathing out, in a long exhalation, see with your inner eye that a string from the ball of rope moves downwards inside your right leg and out through the foot and down in the ground. Wait before you breathe in, use as much time holding your breath as you used to breathe out. Give yourself time to feel that you are in contact with the earth.

Breathe in again, a long, calm inhalation, and imagine the red string coming into your left foot and moving upwards inside your left leg. You experience and see the red rope coming back to the hara chakra. Wait a couple of seconds while registering that you have contact with hara. You are heavy, you stand with your feet solidly fastened to the ground through the floor.

Then you exhale again, at the same time you see the red string moving down inside the right leg and on down into the earth. You register that you are in contact with the earth. You wait before you inhale through the left leg and see the red string move up through the left leg and back to your belly.

Continue this exercise for some more minutes. When you finish, you will feel that you are present in your belly, in hara. This is a good secure feeling. You are in balance, in contact with yourself and Mother Earth. You may want to do this in front of a window, looking out on a tree, a beautiful view or a sunrise. You might also put a lighted candle in front of you while you do the exercises. It is good for us to let our eyes rest on something we find pleasant, something beautiful.

As human beings, we are inseparable from nature, we are a part of it, it talks to us. Bring with you something from nature into your house: a stone that talks to you one day when you are out walking, some branches, cones or moss. Draw beauty and strength from nature and feel that it is a part of you. Everything is a part of the whole.

What do you really want?

Thoughts can be disturbing. They are too numerous, and they repeat themselves.

Around ninety-five per cent of them we have already thought before. Many of them are completely superfluous, they bring nothing new, in fact they are more of a hindrance when it comes to our evolvement and our creativity. They are like background noise which will not leave us in peace. We lock ourselves into them, turning our ponderings and worries over and over in our minds.

They leave no room for what lies inside us and wants to come forth. You should be listening to what is inside you instead. What does your deep wisdom tell you?

One of my clients was very surprised and said, 'I have never even imagined that it was possible to let go of my thoughts!' For him, a grown-up and experienced businessman, this was a real revelation. He managed to breathe deeply and let go of his thoughts. He made a better contact with his deeper self, and was moved and happy to be able to get more energy for both his private life and for his business.

So inhale and now and then permit yourself some absence of thought. In this state, you may discover things inside yourself which have been hidden away for a long time. The child that you were was forced to accept meanings and demands, and this created disturbing thoughts.

Am I good enough? Is this right? Will Mother get angry now?

Something went missing then; it just disappeared.

Meet your feelings with attention and accept them. Get to know them. If you meet fear, consider it. Feelings that you allow and accept will in time lose their sting. It is what we do not know and understand that is frightening.

You may have met these scary thoughts many times and tried to push them away as well as you could, without feeling any better. That is not the way to do it.

I ask you to let go of your thoughts as best you can, and go into the pain, the fear and the aggression. Go into this feeling that you don't want. Inhale deeply, don't run away this time. Inhale deeply again. Feel the pain, the feeling that you cannot stand. Accept your feeling, whatever comes up. If you feel that this is more than you can cope with on your own, find yourself an experienced therapist to help you. Whatever you do, don't put the lid on them again. Don't run away into something that can help you forget. The most important thing you can do for yourself is to get to know what lies deep in you, and clear out the things that hinder you from living life to the full.

The greatest gift you can give yourself is complete acceptance of yourself and love of your inner child. You have been created just the way you should be. Show yourself reverence and respect. You are the only one able to live your whole potential.

If you feel obliged to achieve, you lose the ability to be yourself. Don't be so tied up by honour, admiration and gratitude – what is so important about those things?

Most people think only of themselves, and won't take any notice of you anyway. They are preoccupied with what other people think of them, and use most of their energies trying to be efficient enough, and to have as big a car, house or bank balance as everyone else.

Let yourself be the most important person in your life. How can you give joy to others if you don't love yourself? Many people think that to love yourself is the same as self-centredness. But to accept yourself is to express joy and respect for the work of creation.

Live your own life without wasting time worrying about what others may think.

Be careful about how you use your time. It is your life and it is important to choose what you want to fill it with. Listen within.

What do I really want? Do I fill my time with what is meaningful for me? Rich or poor, young or old, sick or healthy, these things are not important. What is important is to live consciously, to be in the now, to be present, to take responsibility for every thought, every word, every action, and decide within yourself, in contact with your soul, how to behave. If you cannot decide what you really want, it is a warning that you entirely lack contact with what goes on in the deeper levels inside you.

By using the deep breathing exercises you may be able to make contact. You can change your whole life this minute, and you don't need to circumnavigate the globe or change your job or partner. The change happens within. It is our attitude towards life that is important.

Sit down by yourself. Turn off the TV, the radio, the stereo and the telephone. Let silence fill the room around you and within. Light a candle and rest your eyes on the flame, the pure and calming flame.

Inhale deeply and listen within. What is stirring in there? Or you might put a mirror up in front of you. Sit down by a table with the mirror fifty centimetres away.

Put a burning candle beside you, preferably one on each side of you so there is no shadow falling on your face. Sit like this for a long time looking into your eyes. Observe yourself, meet the person behind the eyes. Get to know this person, the child hiding there, this child who needs your attention and your love. How can we understand our children and our fellow human beings, if we don't know and understand ourselves?

Again, I must remind you that if there is too much unrest and fear, you should find yourself a good therapist, but choose to do something, choose to work on it. Do not live your life with all the brakes on.

Once again, 'As your days are, such shall your strength be.' You will find the strength when you have faith.

Believe in it, that is how it is. But we don't learn this at school. On the contrary, we are taught that if we are not good enough, we will get nowhere. So we toil and toil and often we become more miserable, or else we take risks and end up on the other side of the fence. We work on, becoming more and more competent and efficient, earning more and more and forgetting more and more, about what is really essential. The only thing that has a meaning for us is the job and the money.

If we want to change the world, we have to start where we stand. We have to change our attitudes and ourselves. The beginning of the rest of your life is today, and the world is as you are.

We create our world again and again in every moment of time. So let the fairy tale begin, because life is really an adventure. It is impossible to be bored for a single moment once we have opened the door to our inner worlds. But, as I have already told you, it requires an effort from you.

Doubting yourself creates restlessness, insecurity and sometimes an almost paralysing fatigue. We are tired because we are in conflict with ourselves, because there is conflict between our inner wisdom and our rigid personalities. This is the conflict that makes us turn on the TV, and shopping is as dangerous a drug as alcohol or narcotics. It separates us from that which is essential. We waste valuable time in our lives because we cannot stand being alone with ourselves.

We are caught in the net we have spun ourselves, caught in our self-created prisons and our repressed fears, which may become physical pain or illness. We do manifest our lives; we create them minute by minute.

We become incarnate in order to live out our destinies, to walk our planned path through life, the one we decided upon when we were still in the bardo state of life between lives. We wanted then to work for light and love. The bardo state is like a holiday, because everything there is so wonderful and we live surrounded by love. We understand and see that everything is bound together, every one of us is indispensable. Without you and without me, the universe will collapse.

Soul and personality

The very first impulse is the right one. It is the soul's information to you before the personality takes control. When the soul talks to us, it will come at first as small flashes of light. We have to be very aware and attentive to catch them. It takes only a second before the control, the personality, takes over. It fights a desperate battle to be in control all the time. This is what it has been taught, that is what society instils into us. 'You must not do this or that.' 'That is not acceptable.' 'You just don't do things like that.'

Realise that the personality is clever. It knows how to manipulate you, if only you give it time. It does not understand that you would both be better off if the soul was allowed to lead the way. The aim is to make the personality and the soul work together, then you will be whole at last.

Always follow your first impulse. Get used to listening to your soul and do not wait, do not consider. Again this is the personality trying to take over. It wants you where you used to be, that is what is safe, and that is why it is safe. 'Evolution? What do we need that for? We do not know how that might end. No, sit down, everything is fine as it is.' Do you want to sit and ponder over all the things you plan to do, consider back and forth and assure yourself that every possibility is taken care of, that nothing can go wrong? If you do, you will let your life drift away. At the end of your life, when you take time to look back, you will discover that it did not turn out the way it was meant to do. Spontaneity is dead; you no longer have anything to lead you on to the things you have to do. What happened to the little child's dream?

Ask your angel to guide you. Your angel will be with you and bring those you are supposed to help to you, or you to them. They will be waiting for you. At first this guidance might present itself as a vague feeling about something you should do, an urge to go somewhere, write to somebody, or call them. The opposite may also happen; you may get a sense of where you should not go.

We get many messages, but they are often too vague. When we get into the habit of listening, they will become clearer and clearer.

One day I was on my way to a meeting in Oslo and was walking along with strong steps along a street in the city. Then I suddenly got a message that I was to turn around and go the other way. I could not repress a small protest. 'But this is an important meeting. They are waiting for me! I haven't got the time.'

I turned around. The feeling was too strong. I was guided to the left, then straight on, to the right and further along Jernbanetorget towards the train station, and towards a young man. I went up to him, looked into his eyes and put my hand on his chest – or rather somebody put it there.

His eyes were wide open, but he stared at me unseeing. Under my hand I felt a gun. I realised that I had met him before, a couple of years ago. He lived on a farm where I had been taking a seminar. I spoke to him but he did not react. I put my other arm around him, laid my cheek against his and spoke to him, repeating his name again and again. He became sufficiently alert for me to be able to lead him away. I did not get to my meeting that day.

I brought him home with me and he lived there for two days. He told me that everything had gone wrong for him recently and he had decided to put an end to his misery. But now he was able to cry, rage and vent his anger, and then to sleep.

He slept and slept.

At last, he went back to Vestlandet, believing that he would be able to manage school and everything else that had seemed impossible to him.

In our communication with the angels we develop a sense for which we have no word, a combination of sight, certainty, smell and sound. Suddenly we may know the right thing to do.

I have prayed to my angel to be near, and it is. We keep up a dialogue and it often gives me advice about how to act. However, I am not always very quick to obey. I am still sometimes caught up in my personality and think that I know best.

On the occasions when I do not listen, it costs me dearly: the car crashes or the motor stops, something is broken or money is lost. One way or another, things get messed up.

I was caught in a collision once, and I simply had to laugh with resignation. Snow had just fallen and the temperature was zero degrees. I had tried to call for a taxi but could not get one, and I didn't have much time, so decided to drive myself.

An hour before, my angel had told me to take the bus but I did not want to and was sure that I could get a taxi. Now my angel was there again.

'Take the bus!' it said.

'Then I'll be late,' I said and did not want to hear. I went out and got into the car and drove off into the heavy Oslo traffic.

About 300 metres from the place I was heading to, the motor stopped and the car slid over to the side of the road. It parked itself quite beautifully on the only free space on the street.

No, I did not want to walk. It was cold and windy and time was running out. I tried to start the car up again and again but the motor was dead.

Oh, holy simplicity! What was I thinking?

I am the one who is always talking about the importance of being aware, and that day I was absolutely not. I had even gone against the message I had received earlier in the day, and still my angel parked my car for me.

I asked my angel to help me start the car again. This time it started, and we drove on for just a couple of metres when a big van suddenly appeared and drove right into my car.

And that was that. The car was crushed. I had to walk on in the cold and windy weather, and of course I arrived seriously late for what I had to do.

Little by little I have learnt to listen more and to obey. I have learned to use my natural stubbornness to accomplish difficult tasks and to meet challenges instead.

Somebody once asked me, 'Can my angel help me to obtain something that is not good for me?'

To this I will answer yes. It can happen if you are very persistent in your prayer and forget to add that you want your higher will to be heard. Then the angel may fulfil your prayer so you get a negative experience.

Negative experiences are useful. They help us understand what is right for us and what makes us unhappy.

It is clear that we can help family and friends with the messages we get, but they are not always cooperative. Most people find it hard to believe in angels, and many are not willing to accept advice. We prefer to decide for ourselves and know what is best. It is all about faith, and if we don't feel strong in our faith it is difficult to follow advice that comes from something we can't see.

'*You will call about the building site now.*' The voice was clear and insistent.

'What?' I looked up. I didn't want to be disturbed right then. I was busy with tests for some clients, and I was going to Oslo in an hour's time, so this was inconvenient. I knew what it was about and which building site it concerned. Many months before I had been there and looked at the section, not far from my own. My son and his family were looking for a place to build their house and I had stopped there quite by chance one day, letting my dog sniff around a bit while I sat down on a little mound and let my thoughts float. I had played there as a kid.

The cottage which stood there had belonged to a friend of the family, and I had heard that he was dead. It felt good to be there, and it must have been a good place for children to grow up.

Then Erik, who lived in the house next door, came by. I knew him well and we said hello.

'You can forget those ideas, Sissel,' he said. 'Harald and I are going to buy this site and share it between us to get some more space.'

Well, so it had just been wishful thinking. I forgot about it and did not give it another thought. But today the angel was there with its challenge.

'*You will call about the site now!*'

No, not now. Anyway, the children could easily deal with it for themselves.

'No, I haven't got the time. I must finish these tests before I go. Anyway. Erik and Harald want it.'

'Call about that site now!' The message was loud and clear.

'I don't even know who is selling it.' I said this with a sigh, knowing from experience that it was useless. Problems are there to be solved.

The voice never repeats more than three times. I called for information from all the property dealers in Moss, the nearest city. There were eleven of them, and because I had not been very cooperative, I had to call them all before I found the right one.

'Yes, that is correct,' he said, 'but you are too late because it is being sold right now.'

'Then I raise the offer,' I said. Because the angel had told me this was supposed to be, I would have to do my share. I had no time to call the children. Things had to proceed quickly, there was no time to lose.

I knew it would be good for them to live there. They got the building site and my grandchildren now have only got a short distance to come to their grandmother's house, a sanctuary when their mum and dad are away from home. That is very useful in these busy times when most young parents are busy with jobs and training courses and many different activities. It appeared that, without my knowing it, Erik and Harald were no longer interested in the site.

The angels are with us all the time, once we have called on them. Sometimes, but rarely, they show themselves as physical or partly physical beings, and appear as more or less transparent. I feel it very vividly when someone dies and goes over to the other side, and once I had a close and decisive encounter with my own angel.

I had been to a New Year's gathering at Stjärnsund, a spiritual commune in Dalarna in Sweden. Forty people were gathered there, young and old, and most of the time was used for meditation. High, positive vibrations were created, as well as all the good ones which were there before, and during meditation on New Year's Eve I suddenly felt that I was lifted out of my body. I found myself sitting on the arm of an angel. She was at least five times my size and she emanated so much beauty, security and love that I was filled with light and gratefulness. I looked around me and saw light everywhere over and around me, but when I looked down, I was surprised to see a tunnel of light, and at the bottom of it I saw some tiny creatures. They were crawling around. 'What is that?' I asked.

She laughed then – a warm, happy laugh. 'That is the earth,' she said. 'Don't you recognise it?'

Yes, then I saw it. I hadn't realised that she had lifted me so high up. It was exciting to watch them down there. I could see how they were struggling along, many without any aim or meaning. I learned more during that short moment than I would have by listening to a long lecture. She showed me my place in Soon and told me that I should live and work there. She also told me about the way I was meant to work, and then, suddenly, I was back in my physical body. There were many angels around those days at Stjärnsund, and they also followed us home to Norway, which, it later appeared, was very necessary.

We chose the shortest way when we were driving home. It was freezing cold – 32° below zero – and the road through the forest was completely deserted. There were no houses, no people anywhere.

The car we were travelling in was an old one, the engine was making odd noises, the radiator was freezing and the contents of the hot-water bottle on my lap turned to ice. After a couple of miles, we realised that we had embarked on a life-threatening adventure. If the car stopped, we would freeze to death. We kept praying and singing and offering thanks and we were brought home to Norway by the angels. We heard them and felt them.

Just across the border, at first light, the car stopped. Significantly, it happened outside a church. The radiator by then was totally frozen, but beside the church was a little cottage with friendly people who welcomed us warmly.

Close Encounter

Life is everywhere. Everything is movement and rhythm, from the smallest atom to the greatest planet. Everything expands and contracts as if in a rhythmic breath. The atoms in the body are in constant movement; nothing stays completely still.

The planets have their own rhythm, moving in their orbits around the sun.

The oceans ebb and flow, day follows night: movement and rhythm. We civilised humans have less and less contact with the rhythm in nature, the rhythm within ourselves. By removing ourselves from nature and from the divine universe within, we are losing something essential to ourselves, and so too are our children. This is contrary to the premises of life; we are dependent on contact with nature, with the rhythms of sunrise and sunset. To walk in the woods, to listen to the sounds of animals and the wind whispering in the trees, to watch things grow; all this is balm for our souls. The civilised human is engulfed by words and stress. We are left with no time to feel; everything has to happen so quickly.

In our big cities, we see many living dead, people moving about mechanically with more or less empty eyes, and young people restlessly seeking something to help them away from meaninglessness.

Even outside the cities, it is becoming more and more common. Children are not wanted anymore, they are sent away to kindergartens and after-school activities in order to let their parents go on doing their own things. In earlier times, children had to help with work in the home, they were a necessary part of the workforce and they knew and felt that they were needed. Families were bigger, with more grown-ups and elderly people like grandmothers or grandfathers, who had time to answer questions.

There was no TV stealing time away or hindering conversation at mealtimes. On the farms there were often animals needing food and care, giving closeness and warmth.

Communication is important for children. If they are only talked *to* and not talked *with*, there will be little contact and little closeness with their parents. They will experience their parents as distant and will feel unloved. This negative experience will be strengthened if the parents do not communicate between themselves either. We have to understand that life as we live it now can feel very empty and lonely for our children. They have lots of toys, which only take them further away from nature, and most of them have parents so occupied by themselves and their work that they live a life far away from their children.

Even the best television entertainment cannot replace a hand to hold, contact with an attentive mother or father, somebody with time to listen and talk, or walks in the woods with a father who shows them animal tracks and shares his joy in the beauty of nature. No film, no matter how exciting, can replace a mother intensely occupied in creating things with a small child, or who lifts it up and carries it to the window to show it a beautiful sunset.

We must realise that what children have not learned when they are small cannot be seen and appreciated when they grow up.

The result is that too many children grow up searching and seeking for something to give their lives meaning. We see young people doing desperate things in order to feel something other than emptiness. Many of them have never had the experience of being seen, being listened to, being taken seriously, because the parents themselves do not know what it is to have that experience. They have no contact with the depths within.

For many people life is work, food, TV and sleep. In some homes there is no conversation, only empty, idle chatter. I know this from my pupils when I was teaching in school and from my young clients.

Let us bring good conversation back into our homes; it disappears where TV is allowed to dominate. Let us bring back words like love, awe, respect, peace, joy and gratefulness in our conversation around the dining table. Bring those things naturally into the conversation. Soon the dining table will be the only place where we can sit together with the family and have a chance to influence the children. Many people do not even sit down when they eat, but grab something from a food stall while they are hurrying on to the next task. What about the children who grow up in homes like that? Can we see what we're doing to them and ourselves? Where is the closeness between our children and ourselves?

Little by little, our society is becoming so brimful with efficiency that we have almost no time to sit down. 'Clever', 'rich', 'smart' and 'efficient' are words we see more and more in the media when we talk about successful people. Words like 'devoted', 'honest', 'honourable' and 'conscientious' are rarely heard, as if they have disappeared from our language.

I have many young clients coming from homes where they rarely see their parents and where any suggestion of the family gathering at the dinner table is virtually a joke. They laugh bitterly when I ask about this.

It is essential in life for all of us to know that every one of us is indispensable.

We are all cells in the earth's organism; we are all part of a whole, a totality. Without you, without me the universe will collapse. We are all equally necessary for the whole. We came from God at the beginning of time and we are on our way back, through darkness, while all the time we learn and experience, and work our way back towards the light.

When we work with rhythmic breathing and practise it, we can get rid of some of the disharmony within ourselves and get more energy. With rhythmic breath it is easier for us to concentrate, to improve our ability to learn, to heal and to meditate. By sustaining a rhythmic breath over time, we can summon up enormous energy. We become active receptors of prana, the universal energy.

To start practising a good rhythmic breathing, it is important to sit with a straight back. If you slump into a chair with a round back, you restrict your lung capacity and you will tire sooner. If for some reason or another it is difficult for you to sit up straight, you can lie flat on your back on a firm base.

Let your arms rest on your thighs and put the middle finger and the ring finger of one hand on the artery of the opposing wrist. Sit for a while and feel your pulse and listen to it. Then you take a calm and deep breath in order to fill your lungs completely and at the same time count your heartbeat. Count up to six. Have you completed your inhalation? If not, count on until your lungs are completely filled. Hold your breath for half that time. For example, if you inhaled counting to six, you should hold your breath while counting to three and exhale slowly counting to six.

Then you count three before you calmly breathe in again with a good, long inhalation counting to six. Continue in this way. Breathe in counting six heartbeats – hold your breath, counting to three – breathe out, counting to six – pause, counting to three before you breathe in again.

Get into the habit of using rhythmic breathing several times a day, for instance before your lunch break or before you lie down for a rest. It is a very good soporific – your body will calms down into a restful peace.

Stress is one of the worst causes of fatigue and exhaustion, so the time you take for breathing exercises is well worth it. Rhythmic breathing has a very good influence on your health. It helps the inner organs to relax so they obtain the energy to work the way they should.

Human beings are blessed with much greater abilities and power than we suspect. Everything is there for us, for you and for me.

The prison door, the bars and the walls, are all inside us. If we can open them, everything opens up for us, permitting a vibrant, joyful life with God and fellow humans.

Some people remember this and know it, but most of us have no faith in ourselves and don't even think about it. These are things we don't learn about at school or in our communities.

One day in town I went past a young man who was just standing there staring in front of him with a face that was so sad, so very sad. I stopped a couple of metres from him, pretending to be looking into a shop window, and sent him light and love, repeating within over and over again, 'I greet the Christ in you.'

Only a minute or so later, he straightened himself, his aura expanded and his face became less tortured. Then he walked down the street at a confident pace. I often do this.

Once when I was helping collect money for a good cause, I went into a café to see if I could find some generous souls in there. I saw a man sitting at one of the tables who was visibly marked by a hard life, and when I went over to him he asked me to sit down and talk. He was not sure he had anything to give. I sat down and looked into his eyes to make contact with what stirred inside him.

Suddenly he said, 'What are you thinking? Do you think that I am a horrible person who only drinks and wastes away my life?' His face took on a stubborn, irritable expression.

'No,' I answered, 'I greet the Christ in you. We are two souls meeting each other.'

He just sat there for quite some time. His eyes filled with tears and it seemed that something heavy was taken from his shoulders.

We have the power to send light, strength and love to each other. Every thought we produce is energy.

We can see that newborn children have contact with the angels around them. We observe their wonderful ability to wonder, to see, discover and enjoy, being aware of themselves. Some children are able to keep this ability for two or three years, a few even longer if they are blessed with parents wise enough to leave them in peace.

Small children often have imaginary playmates. 'No, this is only something you are making up,' their parents often say. 'You must see that there is nobody there.' But grown-ups who are in harmony with themselves will listen to the children, even if they themselves don't believe in angels. It is better to say, 'Is that so?'

Everything a child says should be of interest to a father or mother. That is how you teach the child to observe and to listen. A child who is told, 'No, you are just dreaming,' or, 'Now you are lying,' will shut off from the wonderful experiences they have with their angels.

Children believe what their parents say. To a small child, parents are the guiding figures, the gods and goddesses.

We have the power to help each other. Remember that you are a soul. The most important part of you is the soul. The human being is a soul with a physical body. The soul carries the body around as it wants. Fill yourself with energy at every inhalation. Yes, you are reading that correctly – *at every inhalation*. Every time you breathe in. If you do that, it will change your life and improve your health, but it takes time to perfect the technique. It requires hard work, even though it sounds simple.

We have been breathing lightly from the moment we were born. We have been breathing just enough to keep us alive, so that we avoid contact with pain. It is as painful for the child to be born as it is for the mother to give birth. Our arrival in the world is connected with fear and shock. We come from a warm womb straight into a cold room, held upside down. We get a blow to the behind to make us start breathing, the umbilical cord is cut, drops are put in our eyes and suddenly we are so totally alone. Because the first breath is connected to so much pain, we often get into the habit of breathing lightly.

Breathe even deeper now. The quality of your life becomes altered if you will only breathe deeply enough. Think of the times when you have been on a long trip on skis or a long walk in the woods. Then you have been breathing fully and deeply for a long time and your whole body feels good. It is not only the joy of being out and enjoying nature that makes you feel alive and gives you this good feeling in your body, but the deep breathing which has filled the blood with oxygen and given new life to every cell. You have been filling yourself with new energy.

So many of us have enclosed ourselves in cocoons because of the terrible shock it was to arrive on the earth, and the loneliness we felt when we were not met with warmth and acceptance. It can be compared to being shut off from the sun. It can seem safe to close up like this, but something essential is missing. Absence of breath means no life. Superficial breath means a little life – we live on the surface. Full, deep breath means full life and full energy – we are in contact with the deeper levels in ourselves.

Manifest your will. Discipline yourself to breathe deeply and fully, and from the first day you will experience a different quality of life. Feelings will surface, and you will have more contact with what is happening inside.

Many people are afraid to feel what is stirring inside them, but why live your life only halfway, with fear and pain cemented into the belly, the back, the whole of the body? Where do you think pain and physical disease come from? Live your life without the brakes on. Dare to be who you are – yourself.

Wanderers

'Things are never bad, it's the way you think about them.'

Epictetus

Many of the people who came to me were in a state which in traditional psychology would be considered pathological. It is my dearest wish that we, the alternative therapists, will some day cooperate with the psychologists. I can count on one hand the psychologists who have sent me patients, and on the other hand, I can even more quickly count those who have been willing to cooperate.

There must be a greater acceptance of the fact that people are more than a physical body and that they must be treated accordingly. Many of the patients who came to me had used conventional medication for a long time before they decided to try an alternative way. They came after having been advised by family or friends.

Mary came to me with her angst and insecurity. She was afraid of most things and could see no light ahead. 'I wish I could die,' she said. 'I have had such a strong desire to die that I thought I would manage to. I have dreadful pains in my legs and I get fatter and fatter. I am always scared of saying the wrong thing. It is so bad that I do not want to go out anymore. I can't stand taking any more medicines, they make me completely lethargic. Everything seems hopeless.'

We had a series of breathing sessions. During the first one, she went back to her youth and re-experienced her stern father and her indifferent nurse. Her mother had died young, and she didn't remember her.

She was rarely allowed to go outside the garden gate and had no contact with other children. She was surrounded by grown-ups till she started school, a year later than she should have.

During the breathing session, she re-experienced her father screaming at her that he would cut off her mouth if he saw her with lipstick on, and that she was to keep quiet when others were talking. She saw herself sitting for hours on a little stool in the kitchen forbidden to move. This was the usual punishment when the grown-ups thought she had been disobedient.

Now, after breathing continuously for three-quarters of an hour, she left her body and lay there for several minutes as if she were dead. She came back with a gasp, which turned into a deep releasing weeping. She was the helpless little girl again, and when the weeping stopped, she lay on her back and floated.

After a while, a peaceful expression came over her, and when I called her back half an hour later she joyfully told me how well she felt and about the wonderful colours she had seen. Two weeks later she came to see me again, highly delighted, and told me that her thighs had lost eleven centimetres in diameter after the first session with me. She had had no pain in her legs for several days. In the second week her legs had started to tighten up a bit again, but after six hours she was free of pain and, what was even better, she felt more secure, needed no more medication and was enjoying life.

Jostein had a general depression. His brother had been attending one of my classes and advised him to do the same. He did not dare to take the whole course, and for the first few times he came only for private sessions.

At first he did not say much. He just told me that he could not enjoy anything. 'The only thing I like is driving very fast,' he said. He had pains in his back after a car accident a couple of years before.

At first impression he seemed a successful man. He was handsome and walked with calm, long strides and he had an open smile. But I did notice that his eyes would not meet mine.

He looked at me when he first introduced himself, but after that he always looked away. I felt sorrow in him and from his aura; he hid away from himself and the world.

So we started breathing, and there was crying, then deeper breathing and deeper weeping.

After the breathing session he lay as if in a deep trance and it seemed that he had forgotten about the weeping. He felt much lighter, but still his body and subconscious would not let go of the memories. Each time we went deeper, and during the fifth session he suddenly got into a former life. He saw himself as a German soldier at the front. He was shot in the side, very close to the spine, and did not die straight away but lay there crying with pain and weeping in despair because he would never see his girlfriend again and because he was lying where no one would find him. It took him a long time to accept his own death. We had to work with it for a long time, but when he got far enough to be able to accept what had happened, and even to see the experience of his earlier lives as positive, his back pains disappeared.

Lilian came to a course that I held in Bauneholm in Denmark. When I saw her, I felt a sure warmth in my body. *I know you*, I thought, but cannot remember from where.

This course, with the breathing sessions she took part in, gave her a boost which changed her life dramatically. She was one of a group of children who had been wrongly diagnosed and wrongly labelled, and she had been sent to a school for retarded children.

This gave her a feeling of inferiority and taught her to become as inconspicuous as possible. When I met her, she was a grown woman. She had been trained as a relaxation therapist, but because she completely lacked faith in herself, she had never practised. She received social security because of bad knees, and had hidden herself away, leading to a lonely life in her little apartment.

She tried to comfort herself with alcohol and her records, and she painted the most beautiful pictures which she also kept to herself.

The light that came into her eyes by the end of the course was very touching. She came to several other courses, both in Denmark and in Norway, stopped drinking and developed her creative talents. She had the warmest hands I have ever experienced and now she used them to help her patients. At last she came to an intensive therapy course in Norway, and a lot happened in those two weeks. We had regressions, and one of them took her back several hundred years to France where she experienced being murdered. It was a painful death; her knees were crushed and she was thrown aside to die. We had to go back again before she was able to forgive the crime, and it was not until then that her knees got better.

I felt certain that we had met in a previous life. We developed a deep, close friendship. She came to visit me every summer and spent several weeks at Lykleungen, my home in Soon. One day, many years later, I had a call from her neighbour to say Lilian had passed away. It had been a quiet, calm death. She had been sitting in her chair with a cup of coffee when she died from cerebral haemorrhage.

I had made an arrangement with Lilian concerning whichever one of us died first, and I took the first plane down to arrange the things that had to be done. I asked two friends, Liv and Tove, who were living with me at that time, to celebrate a service of light at the same time as the funeral.

When I got to Lilian's apartment I stayed there, slept in her bed and meditated in her chair, but I made no contact with her. Then I realised, no, of course, she is at my home, at Lykleungen. She loved to be there and had her own little house in my garden. During my next meditation I asked for contact with her, and she came for a moment as a warm feeling beside me. Then she went back to Norway, to Lykleungen, and she could not be felt at all in the room where her body was lying.

During the funeral. Liv and Tove did as they had promised and celebrated a service of light in my home. While they were sitting there with their eyes closed, Tove felt that she got a loving touch on her shoulder as a farewell. Surprised, she opened her eyes to see if somebody was there, but saw nobody. All the clocks in my house stopped at the exact time the funeral began, and they started again when it was over. Lilian showed herself a couple of times after my return home, mostly near her little house in the garden, like a shadow of light close to the house.

A fortnight later we celebrated another service of light for her, and while I was putting lights and flowers on the altar, I wondered if I should take away a big bouquet of roses which were already two weeks old. The flowers were drooping their heads a little and starting to go brown at the edges, but this bouquet had meant something special to me, so I left it there for another day.

During the service I asked for contact with Lilian and at the same time prayed for her to be taken into the light; that she should walk towards the light and understand that she was dead; that her time on earth was over for this time. She manifested herself to me then as a form of light, and then she left us.

When I opened my eyes, one of the yellow roses in the dying bouquet was filled with new life. It had lifted its head, and stood there as a fresh and full-blown rose, with no sign of brown on the edges.

Once again, a couple of months later, I had a message from Lilian. It was early morning and a blackbird had woken me with its wonderful song.

I was lying in a state of deep rest, my breathing even and deep. I was in contact with some light beings and I did not want to come back. Not yet.

Blackbird! It was the blackbird! I leapt out of bed and ran outside. Blackbird, I have been waiting for you... There hadn't been a blackbird in my grounds for many years, and never one as close as this. It sat there close to the house, just outside the window.

Such rich, fine notes. It moved about, singing for a while by one corner of the house, then by the next, and then back again, just above my head. This happened over and over, all around the house and around me.

And such a tone! I have never heard a blackbird as I did that day, except at Lilian's in Denmark. I had often sat by the window at her place and listened to the blackbird which sang more beautifully there than a nightingale. I have never heard its equal anywhere else.

I had often thought that there must be a link between Lilian and the blackbird. To this day, no other has sung like Lilian's blackbird did on that occasion.

'Lilian! You were here just a moment ago, with the other light beings when I came back from my sleep. It is you, a message from you. This bird sings like the bird at your place.' What wonderful, rich song! The notes uplifted me, reaching my innermost being.

'Thank you, blessed bird. Take my greetings back with you.'

It went on singing for a while longer, mostly above my head, but again and again around the house, and I stood there surrounded by the most beautiful tones. Then it flew away – where to?

It never came back, but the joy stayed with me. Lilian's death released a multitude of images from former lives. Suddenly they were there quite clearly, sometimes accompanied by scents, sometimes by warmth or chills. It could happen when I breathed deep down and just was, or when I was waking up after a good, deep sleep. Sometimes it happened after a meditation. The feeling and the images were there, insistent, expectant:

'You will have to take care of me.'

'What will you do about me?'

'I am part of you, from once upon a time in earlier days.'

Then it happened again. It was early morning and a wonderful stillness filled the house and the landscape. I had been sitting for a long time meditating and was ready to finish, but this was not the time to stop. I was floating away, far back in time. I was in the South of France, standing on the drawbridge of my father's castle with Rodriguez, who was my best friend. We had grown up together and we had just become blood brothers.

My father who treated him like a son had fostered him. We spoke together for a long time that evening and we promised eternal faithfulness to one another. The next day, I was due to leave and be away for a long time, and he was going to stay behind. This was my father's decision and his word was law.

The picture was suddenly blurred and I felt that I was sinking. I could not control it and did not really want to. I wanted to get to the bottom of this. I felt that it was urgent.

I saw myself as a killer. At first it was only an impression, it began to sink in but there were no pictures, not yet.

No, it is not possible. Why... how? But I did not get any answer. It is quiet as the grave, in me and around me.

Then I opened myself to him and I saw him in myself. I prayed to my angel to be near me, and suddenly my heart opened to him.

I forgave him, and myself, and held him. I was filled with love for him, for myself and for everything that had happened. I understood that he could not have done anything else. He felt that he was right, believed in what he did.

Then I did not see him any more. But everything was carried by love – the divine, absolute love.

We returned to the light. Everything around me became light. This experience gave me deeper understanding. I understood even better the secret of acceptance, forgiveness and love; unreserved love for everyone and everything.

Six months later, I was back in Denmark giving a seminar and I seized the opportunity to see a regression therapist there. He took me straight back to the old place, my father's castle. Many years had passed since I left it and I could see that I had aged. I was many years older, and I felt it as well. One image followed another, time did not exist, everything happened so quickly. My father was dead now and my blood brother, Rodriguez, had taken my place. He had also taken my woman. I smashed his knees and let him be carried away.

This life as a knight revealed itself to me many years later, at least in some flashes. The sorrow I felt about what had happened then, that I had a beloved blood brother who betrayed me, and that it was I who had killed him, had stayed like a pain, a sorrow in my belly, through several lifetimes.

Gradually I realised that Lilian and I had had many lives together and I understood even better the deep love that had bound us together.

Later, under treatment by an advanced therapist, I felt that the massage literally penetrated bone and marrow. Simultaneously the therapist touched the crown chakra and the third eye, and I felt that I started to float out of my body. He suddenly thrust his elbow deep down into the left side of my stomach and asked me to breathe into the pain.

It pierced through me like lightning, a pain cut like a string into the region of the heart. I was back in a battle, a fight involving man against man, and I experienced being pierced by a lance.

I realised that I had turned my head, I didn't want to know who killed me. It came almost as a relief. I had had a premonition that this would be my last day, and that morning I had called one of my most trusted men and told him that if something happened to me, I wanted him to marry my daughter and take care of my property. It was written down in front of witnesses.

My killer was just a dark silhouette against the red evening sky. The next thing I felt was that I was being carried home by my men. Eight of them bore me on their shoulders. They were all in full armour. Their helmets reflected the light from the evening sun. I felt the affection and sorrow of my friends before I fainted again. I thought I was dying then, but soon afterwards I saw myself inside the castle. A young woman was kneeling beside me, cleaning my wounds and putting herbs on them. She was my daughter.

I wanted to tell her that it was too late, I wanted to thank her and tell her that I loved her. I also wanted to say that I hadn't been a good father and that I was sad about that. I saw and understood that I had been away from her and the others far too much.

I wanted to speak, but it was no longer possible. I floated up into the light and hung there for a while under the ceiling to say a last farewell and send love to her and to my men, who were standing along the walls. Then I was gone.

Everything turned to light, as it should. Everything was whole, I would meet them again. Now I saw my blood brother, Rodriguez, coming towards me. I saw everything he had been, was and would become.

Then, inexorably, I was back in this life. I felt icy cold, my body felt dead. I could not feel my arms and legs or my body. I felt as if I was nothing but a head, a head that could still perceive the light.

Then I felt my stomach and a ring of warmth started to spread in it. My stomach was there!

I cried and cried. Something loosened deep inside me. While I was crying, warmth and feeling swept back into the whole of my body, into my arms and my legs. Peace filled me. I loved and was loved. Nobody could take this away from me. I was a universe in myself. Everything was and is good for ever.

'Are you all right?' The voice of the therapist reached me, blurred and distant as if through a layer of cotton wool. I opened my eyes.

'Yes, I am. I am so much all right I feel absolutely wonderful.' I laughed and he laughed too. Everything was as it should be.

We were only two small pieces, but we felt like kings.

Reincarnation

'My cat, my kitten, they took my kitten. It was gone when I got back from kindergarten.'

The young man who was lying on the mattress in front of me spoke in a broken, complaining voice. He curled up and cried as if his heart would break. He was a small child pouring out his sorrow, opening up for a wellspring of feelings that had been locked up for decades.

'It was the most precious thing I had. It was soft and warm and it was mine and they killed it… I hated them for it.'

The last sentence came after a long while, and there was an expression of clear surprise in his voice. He did not know that he felt like that, had never thought about it. He had just closed in on himself, cut himself off from the grown-ups. They could not be trusted. He was a lonely child and a lonely young man. His parents had been like big children themselves, not knowing how to take care of him. A friend had persuaded him to try a session with me.

He was afraid and suspicious and did not trust me, but he was desperate. He did not know how to function in life and was willing to try anything that might help him. It was a good breathing session. He reached repressed memories from his childhood. He got through several significant events of his youth and was able to weep out and through what he got hold of, there and then.

It was a lot, and after two hours he said in surprise, 'I have not wept since I was a little boy. I have not been able to. I have been all stiffened up inside, as if I were frozen. I never thought I would be able to cry again. And I cannot remember having been so relaxed. I feel so good. Small bubbles are streaming around inside me, and my feet are warm. They never used to be.'

Rebirthing – breathing that makes you free – is the key to the deepest levels inside us. It is a tool to reach into our repressed experiences. What fantastic, rewarding work this is! I experience it over and over again – people open up like flowers. They breathe into repressed, bad memories, breathe into them and then through them. They meet pain, rejection and sorrow, breathe on through it and realise that they can be better and happier.

Some go through violent experiences, others breathe calmly and quietly throughout as they float in and out of their experiences. For all those who breathe deeply, a change happens.

During all the years I have been working with releasing, liberating breath, breathing sessions, rebirthing, holotropic breathing (all good names for the same thing) I can count on one hand those who did not get a positive result from it. They are the ones who did not dare to breathe deeply enough. They stopped as soon as they felt something happening in their body.

They have never breathed more deeply than necessary just to maintain a minimum existence; they never filled their lungs completely, and they did not dare to breathe more deeply when they were with me. Control was more important for them, and they could not and would not let go of that control.

They preferred to go on as before, regardless of how bad it was. It was familiar, and it was safer to stay in the familiar than to dare try something new. They were scared that their lives might become even worse.

I have never seen anybody get worse; on the contrary, time and again I have seen them get better. The fears we go into will diminish. All the negative things we dare to confront lose their power. The scary things are the ghosts, the shadows we don't want to see, and they grow bigger and bigger.

Throughout my younger days I was paralysed by the thought of torture. The angst made me sweat and I could not bear to think of it. I became physically ill if I saw pictures of prisoners being tortured or if I read about it or heard somebody talk about it.

So, one day in a deep meditation, where I had been breathing continuously for an hour, I went into a former life and I saw everything as clearly as I see the life I am living now. I saw myself being tortured to death. I saw how I was attached to a wooden bench, I saw the colours, how I was dressed, the wet stone walls in the cellar. I saw the others who were there, and felt the physical pain. I died a slow death.

I watched the whole thing with infinite sorrow, and yet with acceptance. It had happened – nothing could be changed except my attitude to it.

I followed myself out of that life and into the bardo state, life after death. I remember having made a decision that in the next life I would work to promote love among humans on earth.

Love is the only thing that can save the earth and its population.

After this experience I had a different attitude towards torture. It is horrible and meaningless, but I now can read about it and hear about it without being sick and without getting tears in my eyes. To the best of my ability I shall, in my own way, work for a better world for all of us to live in.

Only in these very recent years has it become acceptable in Norway to talk about reincarnation. The Church had put a lid on it and taken it out of the Bible.

It was decided to remove all knowledge about reincarnation from the Holy Scriptures, the Bible, at Church Councils in Nicea in the year AD 325 and in Carthage in 397. This was when the canonical text was established and all documents with different views were destroyed.

Much of what Jesus preached, and which makes his teachings strong and full of joy, went the same way. It was too dangerous; it made the people independent of the clergy. It took power away from the Church and gave it to the people themselves.

So we were left with a literary Christendom. Nobody could teach the pure knowledge that God is present inside every human being. The clergy became a hierarchy instead of being God's servants and helpers on earth.

I read the Bible a lot when I was young, but often found something amiss. I had an instinct that there was something wrong, and after a while, I put it aside and started listening to the divine voice within. Then, during an incidental search for informative literature in Strube's Bookstore in Copenhagen, I found G J Ouseley's book and I felt that I had found a jewel.

After that, I could read the Bible again and fill in all that had been removed from it. It became a joyful recognition.

G J Ouseley was a young English priest who in the year 1881 got hold of an old, previously unknown and therefore uncorrected gospel text. This gospel had been safely guarded in a Buddhist monastery in Tibet, where a young man from the Essenes had hidden it. Ouseley translated the Aramaic text into English and called it, *The Complete Gospel*, subtitled 'The Gospel of the Holy Twelve'.

For all those who may be interested, I can tell you that the book has been translated into German and Danish and it can be found at Strube's in Copenhagen, if it has not sold out.

Here we find Jesus as the friend he was, vividly warm and caring, and as the protector of animals. That's where I found the Jesus I remembered from my life as an Essene.

In my present lifetime, I have often looked for love in people's eyes and not found it. I especially expected to find it in people who call themselves Christian, but even there it is rare to find someone who radiates the love we met in those who surrounded Jesus.

I can remember once as a young woman coming home from church and going into my kitchen. I stood with my back to the wall and let myself slide down to sit on the floor. How can people go to communion and not be happy? I wondered. They seem so sad and serious and downward-looking. I tried to smile at them because I loved them, but they looked away. We were singing the words, 'We Christians love our brothers,' but they were not cheerful and they did not show any love for each other.

'You expect too much of people, Sissel,' was the answer I got. 'You cannot expect everybody to think like you.'

Couldn't I? Jesus talked about love, that we should love each other and live in God. Could people believe in God and not be cheerful?

I stopped talking about it because I realised that nobody was listening. Some people were irritated by me, but by far the majority of them were simply not interested. They were not there in themselves, but I did not understand that then.

I continued searching inwardly, into the very depth of my being, to wonder and observe.

I studied nature, animals and people. Most of all I am fascinated by children, and feel a close connection with them.

They are not closed off, they are present in themselves. With them I can *be*. We *are*. I *am*.

After my experiences of seeing myself during earlier lifetimes. I had to start thinking about my attitude towards reincarnation. The conviction that we live several lives here on earth matured in me, and I remember asking my father if I really belonged with him. I was not sure; everything seemed so strange. Then pieces of the puzzle started to fall into place, and as the years passed, I experienced several former lifetimes, both during breathing sessions and in meditation.

During a rebirthing session abroad, I had my most liberating experience using breathing technique. For several days we had been working intensively as a group. We meditated, sang '*Om Namaha Shivaya*' for hours, and helped each other with rebirthing sessions. There was a strong energy build-up in the house.

Two newly trained rebirthers were working with me. They were young and enthusiastic. She was from New York and he was from Berlin, and the night before they had been filled with excitement as they told me all about their experiences during the few months they had been working with clients. They were new, certainly, but they were emanating so much love and joy that I was especially looking forward to the breathing session with them. I felt safe and relaxed when I lay down on the mattress.

I was prepared to accept whatever happened. I was going to breathe through however much pain and fear came up. There was much in me still to be met, I knew that, but this became a very different experience from what I expected.

After breathing deeply and continuously for half an hour, I floated out of my body and further on out into the universe. I was following an ocean of airstreams filled with the most incredible colours. I felt at one with the universe and experienced a wonderful feeling of bliss. I saw myself as a point of light and *I was*. I completely *was*; everything was as one and everything was of God.

I thought, This has to last for ever. I do not want to go back. But, suddenly, I felt strongly pulled down to the earth, to one special place – to a couple who loved each other.

Powers outside me then pulled me down at tremendous speed. Surrounded by pink light, I was pulled into my mother's body. I felt enormously strong and happy, with a faith and a certainty that I was strong enough to manage everything.

Everything was harmony. I had come to my parents in this life. I had been out of the body for quite some time, had been lying there without breathing, and I came back filled with the same feeling of calm and security. I looked at my helpers with a big smile and said, 'I love you. Thank you. Everything is just wonderful, there is no more to say. I cannot explain this.'

They said, 'We love you too.' They looked at me and I saw from their faces that this had been a special experience for them too. Their eyes and their expressions are with me still after all these years.

After the session, I felt that I floated down the stairs to the first floor.

'You look like an angel,' a friend who stood there told me.

'And I feel like one,' I answered. After this, I shall never be frightened of anything any more. I have strength enough for everything.'

During the following years, I often experienced earlier lives. It was exciting, thought-provoking and gave me a greater understanding. It gave me constantly deeper insight in how everything is connected; that humanity is a whole and that we are all walking along an evolving road.

One day a very young man came to see me. He came from a well-to-do home, but grew up with little contact with his parents, and little love.

He had been bought by them, given everything that could be had for money, but not their time. They did not really see him as a person. The parents were struggling on with their own lives. Money was the alpha and the omega in the family. The young man felt completely empty and found life meaningless. He came to ask for help to save his own marriage. He felt that his wife was moving away from him and he had done the only thing he knew how to do, constantly buying her new things without telling her that he loved her. Neither did he give her much of his time. He spent most of his time away from home, as his father had done, and was very occupied with money. Now he felt that his wife had grown away from him.

The minute he lay in front of me on the mattress and I put my hands on his head, I was filled with a deep angst. I almost fell backwards. I felt very cold and for a moment everything was quite dark. Suddenly I knew with deep certainty that this man had killed me in a former life, but I could not see when and where; nor was it important. I pushed it away and did as I always do when I have a client. I prayed God to help me do the right thing, and prayed for both my own and my client's angels to be present with their guidance. Then, respectfully, I greeted the Christ in him. My client lay there with closed eyes and seemed to know nothing of what was going on.

As I was praying, I was filled with love for him and I knew that everything would turn out well. Nothing could disturb our work and the session went by without drama. He was reliving the rejection from his childhood, and began to cry. He came to me several times. We worked through his childhood and he felt better about himself and his marriage, and during that time neither one of us had any contact with former lives.

Later that year he sent his wife to me and I was filled with joy the moment I saw her. I knew her. She had been my daughter once, a long time ago. She had been torn away from me, but at first I did not know how.

Some years later, this young woman and I were on our way to another city to take part in a course in aromatherapy. She wanted to learn about this technique and I wanted to know more about the oils.

It was to become a very special course. Only four people had enrolled, and from the moment we entered the place, things started to happen. My meeting with the leader of the course was also a meeting with an old soul, and we recognised each other.

During the afternoon, I was going to give my client a massage but the moment I let my hands move over her body, she spontaneously went into a former life. She cried hysterically and was beside herself with angst and sorrow. The screaming turned into a child's resigned weeping, such as when all hope is lost.

At the same time, I went into that same life. For me the picture was blurred. I only saw an ocean of flames, lots of smoke and many people close by. I felt a deep sorrow and helplessness and at the same time I was fighting to get my hands free in order to protect her. Then everything became a red fog.

She told me she was my daughter, five years old. She was pulled away from me and held while I was burnt at the stake, and the man who conducted the execution was actually her husband in her present life.

We used the better part of the following night to talk about our violent experience. I had seen most of the same things that she had, and at the same time, but I had not seen who had done the deed. When she told me, I remembered the fear I had felt the first time I saw him.

After the course, I took her home in my car, and when we got there she saw her father in the garden and went to talk to him. Meanwhile I went in to say hello to her husband, who had become more of a friend than a client. The moment he saw me, he got up, his face ashen, and he took several steps backwards, leaning on the fireplace.

'Hey, here we are back again,' I said.

He didn't hear me. He said, 'Sissel, Sissel… but I killed you!'

'Yes,' I said, 'I know that. I have known for some time, but don't be afraid, it is forgotten and forgiven. It was another life and another time, and at the time you could not act otherwise. That was you then and there, and that was how it was. You were one among many who made the decision.'

But he simply did not hear me. He was in a cold sweat. He groaned and looked terrified. 'Only, that is not the worst of it. The child, the little girl!'

'The child?' I asked, as if I didn't know, and looked at him inquiringly.

'The child. I held her back – your little girl!' He sat down, hid his face in his hands and mentioned his wife's name.

Why have I told you this? Because I think it is one of the best proofs of reincarnation that I have experienced. He had never had any contact with former lives at all, nor had we ever talked about it.

The night before, at the same time as I had given his wife her massage, he had been out at a party with friends. He had a couple of beers and suddenly he had gone into a kind of trance. He had been sitting on the sofa, apparently unconscious, and his friends had tried to wake him, but to no avail.

He had sat there experiencing these events with his inner eye at the same time as his wife, in another town, was seeing her mother in that same lifetime die a violent death. The couple had had no contact by telephone, nor had they ever discussed reincarnation together. It was not in accordance with his beliefs, and none of his friends were interested in such things.

It had always been material things, the here and the now, which held their attention.

I have had many signs that I have lived before. I have arrived at places which seemed familiar without my having been there in this life. I would know beforehand what was to be found around the corner. I knew the landscapes.

Some years ago, I went to the South of France with some friends. We were going to the homeland of the Cathars. I had heard a lecture by Sissel Lange-Nielsen about the Cathars, a deeply religious people who had been wiped out by the Inquisition during the Middle Ages. Many thousands were tortured and killed, hacked down and burnt alive, often in big groups at one time.

The lecturer told us about a fortress on top of Montségur, where hundreds of Cathars defended themselves for nine months against a crushingly superior force before they had to give in and go down to the pyre. And suddenly, I was there. I was at the fortress, facing the steep descent, and knew that I was one of them. I had no other reaction just then, apart from sorrow and certainty. That was how it had been. Everything was as it was, part of the plan; it is through suffering that we learn and experience. My consciousness expanded further.

So when I received an invitation to go with Sissel Lange-Nielsen to the homeland of the Cathars, I accepted with joy.

The trip to France became a voyage back to a happy, meaningful life, so filled with faith and joy. While we sat in the bus and Sissel read aloud from her books about the time of the Cathars. I paid full attention. I felt the scent of the flowers and the plants that we cultivated. I saw the people who were around me at that time. The people on the bus became blurred.

Two days before we were to go to the mountain with the fortress of Montségur, I woke up with a feeling that I was incapable of either eating or drinking anything. The others asked if I was unwell, but no, I was well and in good shape. When the others went out to eat, I lay at the back of the bus and dreamed that I walked around and just existed. I felt a sadness and a loneliness that I could find no words for, and a sort of blocking, a barrier in my chest and stomach. It was good to avoid the meals, not have to talk or be sociable. I became quiet, and the conversation around me was just tiresome background noise.

One early morning, we set out for Montségur, through a wonderful beautiful landscape. I sat quite still and was in many ways filled with awe as the mountain arose majestically in front of us, in serene peace. Was it possible that such cruel events had taken place here? I felt empty as I climbed the narrow, steep path to the fortress.

I went ahead of the others. It was important to be able to be alone. The despair, the pain, everything had been lived through before, that time in India when I died, when I experienced several lives and several deaths.

I climbed right to the top of the wall on top of the fortress and looked out over the landscape. I felt that this place owned a part of me. A longing for the people I had lived with was streaming through me, a longing for the community of faith and prayer. What a painful road it is to walk through the dark, back to God – to the light, to love.

An hour later we drove on to the place where we were to have lunch that day, at the home of some 'new Cathars' and for the first time in two days I felt like eating. I felt light and cheerful, and it was pleasant to meet with the others again and enjoy talking with them.

The great *wow* experience came on the bus trip back to the hotel. Sissel was reading again from her book, this time about the customs of the Cathars. One custom was to receive *consolamentum* – a sacrament – before they died, and when a Cathar had received this sacrament, he had to abstain from eating and drinking. This custom was called *endura*.

Something in me had remembered what my waking consciousness had forgotten. Only half a year later I had contact with another life before the Cathars.

For several weeks a wound had been forming on my back, close to the left shoulder blade. It was about four centimetres long and one centimetre wide, and it only got worse, no matter how I treated it. I became more and more convinced that it was a former life trying to force its way through from oblivion. I visualised my acceptance of this, and as well as I could I became receptive to the hidden information. Nothing happened until a couple of weeks later when I went to an international seminar on reincarnation in Oslo, arranged by Rune Amundsen. Among the prominent guests was an American, Winafred Blake Lucas, who gave a lecture on regression therapy.

As we sat there in the lecture room, she led us all together in a regression.

Pang! There I was, back as a twelve-year-old boy among the Essenes. I saw the houses, the golden light, the square I was crossing – a little marketplace. I went towards some sort of tent. It was part of the house, but put up like an awning with canvas on both sides, as protection from the sun. A woman stood there serving food, and I felt loving and warm towards her. She was my mother.

It was a short flash, but all the details were clear, as was the way I was dressed. Some days after this event, I died. I was stabbed from behind, just beside my left shoulder blade.

The Essenes committed collective suicide in order to avoid falling into the hands of the Romans. I had the honour of being among the first to be helped out of that life – it was a quick death.

After the regression, the wound on my back got smaller and a couple of days later it was entirely gone.

Sai Baba

The sun rises from the sea like a ball of fire. The stripe of red on the horizon; the golden light – the magic happens again and again. Every day brings a new miracle of sparkling colours. New life, light, a gift – a new day.

I inhaled, filled myself with energy and light and meditated down on the beach. I was alone with the ocean and the sun. There was no one else to be seen.

I was back in the south of India, in Mahalabapuram, where I sought a time of solitude in order to write.

It was good to be here by myself, I felt at home. I had my hut back, a small, primitive hut sitting on its own down on the beach.

When I came back this time, the hut was closed. It was not used any more and was even more run down than before, but I persuaded them to let me use it. It was good to live so simply, I felt closer to nature. Furthermore, I was there to write and I was doing that, down by the water's edge beneath a roof of palm leaves.

I sent healing to the planet earth, I enclosed it in a violet blue colour and prayed for it to be cleansed from radioactive fallout and environmental poisons. I sent love to the people and the animals. I saw the earth as clean, pure and happy. I saw its people finding the way back to themselves, to their true nature. I received energy from God, from the universe, and sent it on.

I floated in a divine light. *I am*. The sun had risen high in the sky. A new day had begun. I went in to breakfast – my coconut was waiting for me.

I was obviously an exciting feature for the children in the neighbourhood. They sat there close together like birds on a cliff and watched me. They kept a respectful distance – about a metre – as long as I pretended not to see them, but when I looked at them and smiled, they crawled all over me, clinging like bees.

They laughed and asked for ballpoint pens. 'School-pen, ma'am, school-pen!' This time I had brought both pens and tennis balls, and the whole crowd disappeared running along the beach toward the village with their prizes.

The day passed very quickly. It was evening by the sea. From my place on the sand I experienced both sunrise and sunset. Darkness fell quickly. When the sun sank into the ocean, I crawled under my blanket. While I was there I followed the rhythm of the sun, of the light. I kept some biscuits on my bedside table, and sometimes I woke up in the middle of the night and had a short meditation under the starry sky. Then I might want something to eat. I slept profoundly and well. There was more air down there by the ocean, and it was not so chokingly hot. I woke up with a feeling that I was not alone. My torch was lying close beside me and I picked it up cautiously and directed the beam towards a tiny noise from the bedside table. Brown, blinking eyes looked at me. It was a pretty, golden brown mouse. No, surely not a mouse? A rat. It sat on its hind legs holding one of my biscuits in its paws, and for a while it sat there quite still. Then, cautiously, it took a bite, chewed quickly, looked at me and took another bite. I probably didn't seem threatening. I thought, Nice to have you here. Sometimes it can get a bit lonesome down here and you are so pretty and so trustful.

I put out the light and fell asleep to the sound of careful munching. In the morning, there were only paper and crumbs left on the table and there was nobody around. Next evening I put a chapatti on the table. Voila, night food for my new friend. Do you sleep during the day, I wonder? Good night, now I want to sleep. I have been sitting out later this evening. I have been talking to the stars. The sky is so enormous here by the ocean and the stars so plentiful.

Quick, cold feet pattered over my face. I woke up with a start. What on earth was it now? I listened, but could hear nothing. There was the torch by my hand and I searched with the light beam. 'Aha, there you are!'

He was sitting up on a shelf and triumphantly blinking his eyes. I had to laugh. That was the cheekiest thing to do! One simply does not walk over one's friend's face, and certainly not with feet that cold. I turned towards him, but I was apparently a bit too quick and he disappeared into a hole in the wall. Again it was quiet, quiet as a mouse. I fell asleep. Next day was my last down there. I was going to leave very early, at four in the morning, to catch the bus to Madras and then go on by plane to Bangalore in order to go to Sai Baba.

That last night I woke up, as somebody was touching my hair, carefully and lovingly. Yes, I dare say lovingly. Why else should he do it? A friendship had been created, a silent understanding. I had fed him biscuits and chapatti. Maybe he was thanking me. Anyway, this was trust, and I was sorry that soon I had to leave my new friend.

The need for sleep got too strong. I would soon have to get up. I turned around and in a flash he was gone. I prayed to be able to sleep in peace for the rest of the night, and I did. I sank into a deep, good sleep.

'You can come and see me now, Sushila. I am going out for a walk.'

The feeling, the sight, the smell and the voice were quite clear. I saw with my inner eye it was Gita, the wonderful elephant belonging to Satya Sai Baba. She stood there looking at me with her soulful eyes, talking to me, thinking of me, and I laughed with joy and gratefulness. 'Thank you. Thank you, my dearest friend, for this wonderful message. I am coming straight away.'

I was sitting on a stool under a sunroof in a little teashop in Prasanthi Nilayam, Puttaparti. I was enjoying my cup of tea and looking at the donkeys going past searching for food. I paid for my tea and walked towards the village gate, leaving the village and going down the nice wide street leading to Sai Baba's town. There were no people around at that hour. It was noon, the hottest time of the day, siesta time for those who are able to have siesta. I put a shawl over my head and walked as quickly as I could manage in the heat of the sun. Even the stray dogs had curled up in the shadows under a tree or behind a house. I was going to a meeting with a friend, and our feelings were mutual.

Gita was Sai Baba's own elephant, and even before I saw her the first time, I was filled with longing and love for her. When I met her, tears filled my eyes because I felt that she recognised me;

that many lifetimes ago we had been together, that she had been my own elephant.

Her trunk was soft and careful when she lifted the fruits I had brought out of my hand.

That first time there were lots of people thronging in front of the big iron gate. Everybody tried to get as close to her as possible and give her fruit through the bars.

Gita came to the gate every day at the same time and called out, waving her trunk and then lifting it over the gate to accept gifts. Inside, in the garden under tall trees, she had her own house and a servant.

Today, calm and quiet reigned. There was nobody in front of the gate, no one at all to be seen in the street. I looked in through the bars. There was no one there either, but I had my appointment, so I knew she would be there soon.

Two minutes passed and there she was, coming out from her house with her servant by her side. She walked calmly towards me waving her trunk and I lifted my hands as a greeting. '*Om Namaha Shivaya*. Thank you.' What a great joy…

She came right up to the gate, which was opened, and she came out to me, stopped and looked at me and waved her trunk. I put my hand on her.

'Thank you,' I said again. 'What honour you show me. I am so happy. You give me great joy.'

There was something I seemed to remember. I could not grasp it all but it made me happy.

We walked along the road under the shady trees and stopped by a big new gate on the other side. A guard was standing there and he unlocked the gate for Gita and her servant. He did not want to let me in. 'No white people here, it is forbidden,' he said. He lifted his hand and stopped me.

'Can't I come along any further?' I looked at Gita.

Yes, you are welcome to come along. I looked again at the guard. He did not know many words of English.

'Gita has invited me to come on in. Satya Sai Baba knows that it is all right, because Gita says so.' The guard stared at me.

Was it an order from the master? He did not understand the words but he got the meaning, so he waved me in and locked the gate behind us. We walked on. Gita broke off branches from the trees, enjoying the fresh food. We sent thoughts to each other, we were completely aware of each other and felt very well.

I communicated with Sai Baba in the same way. All the questions I wanted to ask were answered telepathically while I was waiting on the square in front of the temple.

I wrote a letter to him once, and he took it from my hand. A short while later his answer came back telepathically into my thoughts.

One day during my first stay there, I was placed in the first row. I sat very close, right in front of the temple, and thought that I would be able to meet him personally.

We sat there for hours on end in the burning sun, in a temperature of 38° in the shade. I have never ever been so tormented by thirst as I was that day. My throat was dry. My whole body seemed dehydrated, I could barely stand it.

When this is over, I thought, I shall lie in the shade and drink and drink, I can't bear sitting here any more. But I still didn't give up. I had been sitting outside waiting for a couple of hours and then got a seat in the front row, and I had sat there for at least another hour. I stayed seated. Baba came and walked along the first row.

As he came close to me, five other women stood up with outstretched arms and letters in their hands. He lifted his hand and waved them down. That was no way to behave. He left us and went over to the other side where the men were sitting.

I sat there, surprised and a bit disappointed. I was so certain that I would make contact with him that day. We stayed on for another half an hour, then darshan was over and Sai Baba entered the temple.

Everybody got up and the square emptied slowly as the thousands who had been sitting there left. At last I'll get something to drink, I thought. I felt close to fainting but still I sat there and at last I was all alone. I addressed Sai Baba through my thoughts. 'I was sure that you would come to me today. I sat there waiting for you.'

I got an answer immediately. 'If you are willing to wait for me, I will come to you.'

'Yes, Baba,' I replied. 'Even if I have to sit here for six hours, I shall wait for you.' At that moment my thirst disappeared. I suddenly felt cool and well and not at all thirsty.

Half an hour passed, and then he came out of the temple and stopped right in front of me. I bowed down and put my hands on his feet. All conversation between us was telepathically, words were superfluous. After a while – I do not know how long – I pulled back my hands and saluted him and he went away. To touch the feet of a master is called *padanamaskar* by the Indians. It is a great honour and is considered a blessing.

Outside the temple area, flocks of people surrounded me. They were watching the scene from outside. 'Oh, how lucky you are! May I touch you?' They wanted to have their share of the blessing.

I have very good memories from Sai Baba's place. I have seen him perform miracles. I have visited his magnificent hospital, where everybody gets free treatment, and the villages he has built for poor Indians. He has done a great deal for thousands of people. He is a great avatar.

From Prasanthi Nilayam I travelled on to Delhi, spent a couple of days there with friends and then took a plane to Ahmadabad in Rajasthan.

I had been invited to Brahma Kumaris, a spiritual university on Mount Abu.

Four years earlier I attended the congress of Women for Peace at the same place, together with 300 women from sixty-four countries.

Mount Abu is a magnificent place high up in the mountains, with the most wonderful and powerful yogis, all women. Meditating with them produces a power so great that I have no words for it.

When we were seated on the plane to Ahmadabad, I discovered that I was sitting beside a monk. I looked at him sideways, then I took up a book and started to read. I did not want to disturb him, even if he was sitting on my left side. Monks should be left to their exalted peace. But what is so special about someone sitting on my left side? It always turns out to be a person who will be important to me. It happened that time too.

He spoke to me, and the trip became a great new experience. He asked about my work and told me that he had come from the Himalayas where he had been meditating for three months. He was now on his way back to his own temple. I asked him if he knew the place I was going to. 'Yes. The women who live there sometimes come to us to meditate,' he answered.

I knew that I was talking with a master. He radiated peace, security and wisdom, and during the last part of the flight we meditated. As we went in for the landing, he gave me his card.

'Come to us the next time you come to India,' he said. 'You can live in our ashram, take part in our meditations and use our library for your studies.'

He was sitting on my left side. The last time I travelled by plane between Ahmadabad and New Delhi it was Mother Theresa who sat there.

Postscript

'Write a book,' the astrologer said.

Now it is finished – the book about a life – my life so far. Many readers are sure to recognise things from their own lives; many will have experienced similar lessons in their own ways. But there is a special power in knowing that we all live in order to learn. I have realised that again and again in writing this book.

What was hurtful and difficult has helped me to grow – both as a human being and as a soul.

Things which were joyful, exciting and funny have nourished my faith and given me strength to continue.

Thanks to all of you who helped me to grow.

Thanks to all those to whom I was allowed to pass on something precious.

Thanks to all my clients and pupils, who taught me so much.

Thanks to the loving force which governs us through life after life on our voyage back to reunion with Eternity, with God.

Soon, Norway